Facebook Marketing For Beginners

Master Social Media, grow your brand, attract new customers, and raise your sales and profits. The Ultimate Beginners Guide to Advertising (2022 Crash Course)

Table of Contents

INTRODUCTION

Welcome to Facebook, where you can reconnect with long-lost acquaintances and advertise your own company in as little as 10/20 minutes every day.

The online social graph — that is, every person's chart on the internet and how they are related — is undergoing a dramatic transition. It is the Worldwide People's Internet, a mirror and extension of our offline social network — our friends, family members, classmates, parents, teachers, neighbours, and acquaintances that matter to us, influence us, and for whom we live.

The online social network allows us to be stronger, more successful, more productive, and more content doing what comes easily to us - expressing ourselves and transacting and connecting with people over the Internet. Information taken from social networks, such as where individuals are from, what they are interested in, and who their friends are, may then be used to customize, private, and precise commercial relationships.

For simplicity, I'll call this "Facebook 2021," although I'm referring to the wider phenomena of social networking that is emerging on the Internet.

We currently live in a different world than we did a few years ago, thanks to the fast growth of technology. College students, except for professors and possible employers, now solely use email to communicate — they speak about what they had for breakfast and send Facebook messages. However, college students are not the only ones who are impacted.

While Facebook was founded outside of office hours, its influence stretches well beyond our identities. Facebook statistics have repeatedly demonstrated that adults aged 35-49 have witnessed the highest gain in viewership numbers over the past year.

260,000,000 and Still Counting

On Facebook alone, over 260 million individuals are currently signed in, checking their profile, talking with peers, contacting businesses, sharing vital information for you to better understand them, and learning about themselves in return. You must be where your customers are as a businessperson, and consumers spend a lot of time on social networking sites like Facebook and Twitter.

From its modest origins as a basic online directory for Harvard University students, Facebook has gone a long way.

It currently has 1.11 billion users worldwide, providing a large market of prospective consumers and customers who can serve enterprises of various sorts.

Have you ever considered using Facebook advertisements in your overall marketing plan as a company owner? If you do, you're on the correct route.

According to a **Syncapse poll,** "85 percent of brand followers on Facebook are advocating items to others."

With the introduction of Facebook, the social networking site with over a billion active members, Internet marketing took a new direction. It is currently the most popular marketing platform for companies of all sizes. According to marketing experts, the success of Facebook marketing may be linked to its adaptability and capacity to reach a large audience. Marketers may use Facebook to increase brand recognition among millions of registered users and prospective consumers. Even in 2020, Facebook is the world's biggest social network.

Only a few hundred million individuals took part in **Mark Zuckerberg's** social network effort a decade ago. A decade ago, no one could have imagined Facebook's worldwide success.

Is there anything that can be done to slow the rate of rising? Do you think anything will stymie Facebook's growth over the next five years? The surprising answer is "almost probably no," since Facebook is here to stay. Any social network or online platform with a significant user base will almost certainly not die, but will instead evolve.

Several digital marketers utilize Facebook to sell their goods to the worldwide population, and there is no simpler place to advertise than Facebook since it is used by everyone's target audience 24 hours a day, seven days a week. You may be asking, though, how to tailor marketing to Facebook users.

One of the biggest features of Facebook advertisements is that its authorized advertising platform enables you to target specific people based on age, location, ethnicity, hobbies, and so much more! Because the foundations of Facebook marketing are so straightforward, I enlisted the help of an online Facebook marketing specialist to offer you instructions on how to utilize Facebook.

People of various ages utilize Facebook, which has a minimum age of 13. There are currently no publicly accessible data on Facebook's most popular age groupings, but hundreds of research have indicated that the 1829 age group is the most likely to fit you. As a consequence, persons aged 65 and over are unlikely to utilize it frequently.

Are you still persuaded? "How do I get started?" is the next important question you should be asking yourself right now. I've got an answer for you.

The Complete Guide to Facebook Marketing in 2021: How to Use Facebook

We've previously demonstrated that Facebook marketing is (very) advantageous to any size company. Before proceeding with the remainder of this advice to increase your Facebook marketing success, keep the following items in mind:

What is the purpose of your reading this book?

This book is meant to assist you in comprehending online social networking and its ramifications for your company. The following situations may ring a bell:

You see the significance of online social networking, but you're stumped as to what to do about it.

You use Facebook in your personal life but are unsure how it will integrate into your business life.

Your boss has directed you to set up a Facebook profile for your ASAP company, but you have no clue how or what to do.

You're the boss, and you're curious about the phenomena of social networking and what it implies for your business.

You want to discover how actual companies utilize social media to attract leads, engage new audiences, and transform consumers into salespeople.

You understand that who you meet on social media has a lot to do with whether you're seeking employment, passing up a bargain, or going forward in your profession.

You are continuously pushed to accomplish more with less and to utilize the power of your networks, the networks of your colleagues, and the networks of your customers to make the task simpler, quicker, and cheaper.

This book is based on three essential assumptions. First, organizations are social by nature because organizations are only as good as their people, and people are social by nature.

Personal ties in business have always been crucial, whether they be between a salesperson and a customer, a recruiter and a candidate, a vendor and recruiting employees, or other colleagues.

Furthermore, suggestions and reviews from individuals you know and trust may have a big effect on your buying choice. Finally, research suggests that poor ties, rather than the tightest circle of friends and family, carry the greatest social capital in the corporate environment.

To build and execute an effective Facebook marketing plan, you do not need to be conversant with every Facebook function. This book will teach you all you need to know about marketing on Facebook. Don't worry if you're worried about not knowing enough about Facebook's features; you'll learn all you need to know in subsequent chapters.

While understanding how to utilize Facebook is essential for your company, you need also learn about your clientele and the demographic you want to attract. Facebook's layout and restrictions are known to vary, but as long as you know whose attention you're targeting, you'll find it simpler to respond to these changes and guarantee that the rest of your fans continue to view their news feeds for alerts.

The methods described in this book are the same ones I've used with excellent success. I researched to guarantee that the tactics you'll be learning have been tried, tested, and proved to work.

Chapter 1:

GETTING AROUND FACEBOOK: THE BASICS

Starting Out

First and foremost, congrats! If you're considering joining or are currently a member, you're a part of one of history's most rapidly expanding and biggest social networks. Millions of individuals have similar interests, hobbies, job objectives, and pretty much everything else. To locate all of those buddies, networking opportunities, and events, you must understand how and where to search.

You must also devote time to establishing your Facebook profile, so let's get you up and running as soon as possible so you can take advantage of all of Facebook's wonderful features.

On Facebook, you can get from 0 to 60 in only 11 steps.

Let's get together on Facebook. These 11 steps will help you get your profile up and running in less than an hour:

Spend a Few Moments Getting to Know You

You're either entering a new universe or returning to a familiar social network where you'll be spending more time. It offers a plethora of features, many of which we shall go through.

Submit a Self-Portrait

We'd want to learn more about you. When someone searches for you, they are considerably more likely to interact and remember you if they are greeted with a beautiful image. Furthermore, if they don't have a picture, it might be tough to identify the folks you're searching for, particularly if they have a common name. As a consequence, a profile picture is required. Regardless, one of the reasons you're on Facebook is to maintain great personal ties while also networking.

In this aspect, images are quite valuable. On the marketing side, an image humanizes the name. It enables customers, purchasers, and supporters to contact you directly and know with whom they are speaking.

Please don't post anything obscene. Facebook is not the greatest location to publish inflammatory photographs, and the network's regulations are strictly enforced. Why would you want to upload an offending picture to a network you don't control in a world where everything you do becomes a permanent record?

Please provide a picture of yourself that accurately portrays your personality. The most common sort of profile image is one of oneself, either a headshot or a full-body selfie. This enables you to concentrate on yourself and eliminates the need for others to assume who you are.

It's also worth noticing that the profile picture in search results and elsewhere on the network is significantly smaller. It will be more difficult to determine what is going on and which person you are if there are other people, animals, or objects in the shot. Some individuals, however, do not want to be known or recognized in a search, so instead, have fun sharing a picture of an animal or a place.

Avoid using group images as your profile picture since it will be difficult to see yourself in them, particularly if someone has never seen a photo of you or met you before.

Finish Your Profile

We recognize that this looks to be time-consuming, yet it is one of the most successful methods of finding individuals. If you accept my offer of friendship, it will be the shortest method for me to meet you. Part of Facebook's ever-expanding applications, such as those for iOS, Palm Pre, and Android smartphones, will access some of this data to help keep contact lists up to date.

You are not required to complete all of this; simply answer the questions that you are comfortable sharing. If you don't want your entire contact information shown, that's understandable. If you don't want to, don't reveal your political views. However, take as much time as you need to discuss with you.

You get a week to tinker with your Timeline before it is launched, or you may put it anywhere you want right now.

The first thing you chose is the cover, which will be a huge masthead picture of a great occasion in your life.

To change the cover picture, swipe over it and then click the change cover icon. You will then see a gallery of images open up, and you may select to go into your galleries and search for a suitable image. Once you've chosen which picture works best at that size and how you want to depict yourself, you may want to experiment with others. The question is whether or not this is a professional scenario. Who are your blood relatives? Is it your big day? It all depends on how often you utilize your profile.

The Show Event button has led you to a hidden list of all your messages and events since your first Facebook action. You may adjust an article's or story's privacy settings, remove posts, and do other things.

Start Making Friends

Making Facebook friends with someone is the most usual approach to communicate with them. These individuals may be family members, friends, employers, business partners, or anyone who wants to engage for many reasons. There is no "proper" quantity of friends you should have. You should not concentrate on the number.

Continue to seek out and engage with intriguing individuals as much as possible, many of whom you already know. Facebook is a fantastic medium for creating alliances, personal and professional networking, and interacting with old friends, family, and co-workers.

One of Facebook's most serious problems is the loss of new members who are unable to interact with other users. There are, however, various methods for finding individuals to connect with on Facebook.

Import contacts from AOL Instant Messenger (AIM) or Windows Live Buddies.

Facebook remembers searches based on the educational and job information you provide in your profile. You may, for example, click to do a search with you for everyone who graduated from high school or college.

You may also search by heading to your profile and clicking on the name of your school or company.

When your friends start accepting requests from their peers, Facebook encourages them to recommend new friends to help you grow your network. This is only possible in the early stages before Facebook feels you've established a solid network.

Facebook will offer friend suggestions based on shared connections, comparable interests, and so on as you extend your network. This is an excellent method to meet new individuals. If you haven't discovered each other yet, you might be following each other on other networks and utilizing the methods described above.

Add More Images

Uploading a profile picture or two is insufficient. We'd want to learn more about you. We'd want to see more than just your headshot and the information you've supplied. Another alternative is to build picture galleries and publish them on Facebook.

Create your first Facebook picture albums by gathering a handful of your favourite images. The majority of people, including ourselves, look to images of individuals to learn more about them. We'd want to see where you live, how you spend your time with your children, what makes you giggle at work and anything else you'd like to share.

By enabling you to explore your computer's hard drive and choose all or a specified selection of photographs, Facebook makes it easy to share a huge number of photos at once. You may also post straight from your phone to Facebook, or utilize photos if you have a Mac.

Include a video or two.

Have you had a great video from the holidays or from last Friday night when you were out with friends? Set one over there. We may never have met in person, but by sharing photographs and videos, we can connect with you and match the words on the screen to your personality.

What if you don't have a single video to work with? Start creating 'em. Begin documenting some of the chaos you're generating using a webcam, iSight (if you have a Mac), phone, digital camera, or Flip camera. In the same way that you can add friends to pictures, you can do the same with images.

Try to keep the video around 3–5 minutes long as a bit of advice. Everyone is tremendously busy, and the longer the film is made, the less likely it will be seen, shared, or even written about. Keep it quick and enjoyable!

Send Your First Status Message Using the Publisher Tool

Updating your status tells us what you're up to, what you're talking about, and how you intend to share what interests you, such as ideas, connections, photographs, videos, and questions. In actuality, you are not required to modify your record 487 times every day.

While updating Twitter 20+ times per day is optimal, updating Facebook a few times per day is fine. Updating your status allows you to remain in touch with pals. Allow your friends to provide input and like or retweet the item you shared when your status shows in the News Feed.

Install the Facebook Mobile App.

Are you a part of the increasing group that utilizes a mobile device such as an iPhone, BlackBerry, or Android? If this is the case, you should install the Facebook app on your smartphone.

Go to m.facebook.com to access Facebook's mobile version. This allows you to contribute new material, such as images and videos, check your profile, see what your friends are up to, and explore a range of other applications while on the road. We would use Facebook considerably less if it weren't for the mobile app. This enables us to generate material and convey our activities even when we are not near a gadget or an Internet connection.

Begin Communicating with Your Pals

Facebook enables us to continually develop material to share what we are up to, and this offers you an excellent chance to interact with friends, family, and others you meet.

Use this to your advantage. Keep a lookout for your pals as they post their images and videos while you go about. Look for some websites to share with your colleagues. However, a word of caution: do not use your friends' "personal" Facebook profiles. It's not necessary to reply to or like anything they post. This will not only irritate you, but it may also look dishonest. You'll be well on your road to success if you write on a few topics every day.

Have a good time and start exploring!

What you can do most is an attempt to have fun. You're less inclined to utilize it if you're not having fun. That is something that none of us want to do. You're reading this book to learn how to utilize Facebook more effectively for personal and business objectives. If you don't like the first few stages, everything that follows will make you want to run about with scissors.

Take your time, get used to how things operate and have fun on Facebook. It may consume a significant amount of your time if you want it to, which is OK. Remember that communicating, engaging, and establishing or reinforcing confidence is all important. That is only possible if you put in the effort, have fun, and are honest throughout the process.

Furthermore, it is an investment in your future by enabling you to create personal and professional ties with people, rather than "wasting your time."

While those 11 steps may not cover everything you'll face when you join up for the first time, they will help you feel more at peace sooner rather than later.

Pages and Groups

You can use Facebook to establish, find, and join groups based on themes, goods, companies, celebrities, and just about anything else you can think of. Look up your favourite hobbies, songs, or companies. Consider becoming a follower if you have a Facebook account. Not only will you join a group of similar-minded individuals with whom you may interact in many ways, but it will also be connected to your profile, enabling others to see where you prefer to hang out on Facebook and what you're interested in.

Another excellent program that some people use is Notes. Facebook claims that "You will write notes on Facebook Notes to share your life with your friends. You may tag pals in postings, and they can also make comments."

This may seem comparable to MySpace's blog capability, which was widely utilized but never truly resonant in the manner MySpace's creators anticipated. To see your friends' notes, go to www.facebook.com/notes/. If you haven't used Notes in a while, you may need to hit more to locate it in the left menu.

Although many people utilize Facebook Notes as a blogging platform, it is not advised since there are considerably better professional sites available, such as WordPress, MoveableType, and TypePad.

Search

As more individuals started making money on Facebook, it became evident that the regular search option would not be sufficient. Initially, Facebook Search simply enabled you to search by name for people, courses, or websites. For example, none of the data submitted during status updates could be searched. Twitter's greatest major edge over Facebook has been this.

In 2011, the search engine optimization (SEO) market was valued at $19 billion and dedicated SEO bloggers and conference presenters started discussing Facebook Search optimization seriously. The field is simply going to become bigger.

Other websites may be able to help you with your Facebook search. Greplin (greplin.com) is a fantastic person, private social search tool after you give it access to your social streams. OpenBook was intended to show how few individuals were aware that their status changes were public. It may also be beneficial for product research.

Keeping Friends and Friend Lists Organized

The Friends feature enables you to organize your friends into different lists. This is particularly beneficial if you've acquired a few buddies. In addition to some of the easy lists and searches that Facebook has already built up for you, you may arrange your friends into whatever category you wish. This is particularly beneficial with the improved privacy options for status updates and information sharing. If you've made segmented lists, you may opt to share just particular alerts, photos, or data with each one.

As a consequence, if you don't want your college friends to see the business news you'd want to share with your professional connections, they won't. This also implies that your supervisor will be unable to see your Vegas images.

Many individuals choose to select their family members, which you may do by heading to Profile and choosing Edit Profile. You may even add the intended kid now if you like. Make sure you designate who may view your family connection in your Privacy Settings choices.

Messages

Like many other social networks, Facebook offers its private messaging service. You may accomplish this by going to the top of your computer and clicking on the Inbox tab.

After that, you may send Facebook messages to any of your friends. Facebook, like the Publisher tool, enables you to add links, photographs, videos, or other updates to your program (depending on the actual application).

This messaging service is now part of Chat. Conversations will display in your Conversations area when you chat with someone. There is another mailbox that few people are aware of. This is where Page alerts are delivered.

That's both good and bad; as a Page Manager, you're better off delivering News Feed to your followers, but as a user, you'll receive less spam than with standard emails. If you choose, you may also add emails to your messages.

On the blogosphere, there has been substantial debate over whether Facebook's messaging system would render traditional email obsolete. We think this is unlikely because many companies will be loath to give up domain-branded email, and because not everyone online is on Facebook, even in areas where Facebook is most popular.

Account configurations

Other features of your Facebook account are regulated in Account Settings (see Figure 1.26): you may pick and choose what you wish to share from your profile. This section has a variety of choices, and you should take the time to modify them to your preference.

Set the URL for your username.

Set the sorts of updates you want to receive and how you want to receive them.

Change the number of programs that have access to your account or uninstall devices.

Set up mobile messaging systems.

Use your money to buy Facebook shares.

Consider how marketers could utilize the information on your profile.

Chapter 2:

ESTABLISHING A BUSINESS PRESENCE

A business may create a good Facebook page in many ways. If you're a business leader, you may be asking why any corporation would desire a platform on a social network that looks to be so personal. Go someplace else if you don't want to fish in a pond that is alive with 800,000 new fish every day. Of course, we mean it mockingly. We recognize that some companies are wary about using Facebook for business.

Is it a personal or professional matter?

Facebook has been largely viewed as a personal social network for the bulk of its history. On Facebook, you may let your hair down and communicate with your employers, family, and close friends. You share pictures and videos from recent travels or your child's first steps. You share your thoughts on a range of issues, such as your favorite pizza toppings or who or what is upsetting you today.

When it came to business networking, there was LinkedIn. On LinkedIn, you may upload your CV, make recommendations, start a group for your customer, product, service, or industry, and do many other business-related tasks.

The problem is that Facebook is gaining popularity at such a quick rate that it is impossible to ignore. And a growing number of professionals are using Facebook to network.

Some businesses allow LinkedIn access from the office but not Facebook, Twitter, or other social networks.

You may be asking why we are discussing personal and professional connections. Isn't it true that everyone maintains a distinctly personal and business life?

When you're with your family and friends on the weekends, you're a different person than when you're sitting across from your boss, clients, or suppliers in the boardroom. Right? Right?

We may all interact on a personal level using this strategy, which may contribute to professional cooperation. After all, at our core, we prefer to conduct business with people we know. We have trust in our friends and anticipate their help. We would never intentionally insult, injure, or hurt our friends. As a consequence, when we conduct business with friends, we tend to work more diligently. In general, it's more pleasurable and less complicated. Facebook is a fantastic tool for connecting individuals and companies.

Keep in mind that the Facebook guidelines advise you to do commerce using Sites rather than Profiles. If you already built a corporate profile, you may now convert it to a page. Please keep the following in mind before proceeding: Friends will become fans, but none of your stuff will survive the changeover, including all of your photographs, images, and posts. However, it does not update the vanity URL or email address, and the previous URL is no longer functional.

Establishing a Corporate Facebook Page Aside from determining whether or not to join Facebook and merge your personal and professional life, consider developing a Facebook brand presence to assist humanize your business. Facebook is a social networking service with a highly personal vibe. In a social atmosphere, people admire other users and esteem products that have a personal feel to them.

The sorts of material you select to offer on a Facebook Page or Group may illustrate that your firm is much more than a logo. You can unveil all of the fantastic individuals that make up your firm by peeling back that logo.

Facebook is a thriving community with admirers of your business, leadership, product, or service. If you're shaking your head and shouting at the top of your lungs because you don't have any fans, remember that your prospects, customers, and future fans are all on Facebook. By creating a Facebook presence, you can locate and activate these followers by providing them with a community in which they can communicate with one another and with your brand. You must accept that the days of requiring your prospects, customers, and brand followers to visit a website of your choice are gone.

Yes, you may still direct traffic to your website and convert visitors using a contact or informative form. Corporate websites continue to be quite valuable.

With Facebook's expanding popularity, it makes sense to build a company presence there. At the absolute least, having a rudimentary Facebook presence might make it more difficult for others to claim your brand on Facebook — anyone could build a Page named after your company and portray it in ways you don't desire. Because Facebook contains hundreds of millions of pages, it is impossible to monitor all new pages properly. If you're still not convinced about the value of having a Page, consider this: Facebook has eclipsed Google as the leading source of the traffic to major websites.

How do you get started now that we've convinced you that you need a corporate image? What should you be on the lookout for? What if your brand name is stolen? Is it possible? What if someone makes a bad comment about your Facebook page? Is that anything that will happen? What is the rate of return on our efforts? How long will it take for this to be useful?

All of these issues occur when firms contemplate launching on Facebook.

You are not alone if any of these ideas have occurred to you.

Pages on Facebook

Pages are "a place for any prominent person or organization to engage a discourse with Facebook users... a public profile that lets people connect to what they care about," according to Facebook.

Facebook Pages are used by musicians, artists, sports teams, corporations, media, non-profit groups, and others.

Because Facebook had recently released Fan Pages, which appeared distinct from ordinary accounts, it had limited alternatives. As more individuals joined Fan Pages, Facebook rebranded them Pages and updated their design to seem more like ordinary profiles. Pages need the user to configure menus, attach basic information, and test if fans may post on the site, contribute photographs and videos, and implement other security restrictions. They even provide you Insights, which are metrics (information, fans, and posts) that personal profiles do not have.

One of the most major updates to the Pages was the introduction of the Facebook Markup Language (FBML). FBML may be used to change the appearance, feel, and behaviour of Pages in addition to their other features.

This is now possible with iFrame applications. Create a Facebook Page The first step is to establish and classify your Facebook Page. Begin by going to the Facebook home page and clicking on the Pages link in the left-hand menu.

This will lead you to a certain portion of your Pages. You'll see a collection of Pages here if you've made them or become a Pages Admin. This dashboard view shows alerts, total likes, and the number of active fans per day.

Choose the most appropriate category for your page: a local company or site a company, organization, or institution

Brand or product

Whether you're a musician, a band, or a prominent personality,

Community for Entertainment

In any case, you will be requested to submit further information when you click. For example, a local company or site may seek address information.

Then, enter your organization's name. Please double-check that this is the name you want to show on your Facebook Page.

Once a name has been entered, it cannot be changed. Your only choice is to remove it and begin over (trust me, from experience many businesses know that). After you have carefully picked and written in your name, you will be able to create an electronic signature to confirm that you have the permission to build the Page.

You are now ready to start working on your page. Before exposing your Site to the rest of the world, you may spend time naming it, customizing all of the tools, and fine-tuning it to your tastes.

Configure settings

Other choices about personal profiles may also be customized on Facebook. As you move through the pages, take your time and tweak the settings to your taste. In the initial look of your new Page, there are six stages available: Include a picture.

Invite your Facebook contacts.

By importing contact information, you can keep in touch with your fans.

Distribute status updates.

Use a like box to promote the page on your website.

Configure your phone so that you may update the page from wherever you are.

Put your logo here.

Because your Facebook profile is set up as an extension of your firm, your default picture must be your corporate logo (or a headshot if you're a lone entrepreneur). The width of this logo is 200 pixels, and the height is 600 pixels. Choose the thumbnail with caution, since this version will appear next to all of your status updates.

Upload Photographs

Do you have any images of your business's offices, staff, or anything else? Make a few picture albums and distribute the photographs to everyone. It's worth remembering that you're seeking to humanize your organization as well as develop a brand identity on Facebook. One of the easiest ways to do this is to display the personnel and actual office surroundings that enable the organization to function regularly. If your workspace needs an update, this may be an excellent reason to change things up a little.

Make an archive for any photographs of your items or software screenshots. Each picture or screenshot might be accompanied by a short explanation.

Submission of Content

Are there any behind-the-scenes customer testimonials, product samples, project material, advertisements, or interviews? Use the publisher tool to upload them to your Facebook Page. It takes longer to upload films than it does to post images. However, you may share other types of material with your clients, purchasers, admirers, and even staff. If your company website doesn't already contain all of these videos, your Facebook page is a wonderful way to gather photographs from across the web. Many websites do not have the Videos option in the left menu, thus you may need to go to Edit Video Page, Applications, Edit Video Settings, and then choose (add) next to Open.

Pages' Helpers

Apps are the new moniker for some of what was formerly known as Tab windows. Even the links in your left navigation to Photos and Videos are referred to as apps. On Facebook, there are many more applications to pick from. Each Page form comes with a set of apps pre-installed.

A band website could have a music player, video player, discography, ratings, competition dates, and a discussion forum, for example.

There was once an authorized list of applicants, but Facebook eliminated it. Facebook now expects you to be able to locate apps using the search tool. You may use several programs to increase the speed of your Facebook page, such as:

If you operate a restaurant, you can utilize Open Table or Zagat.

If you or someone in your business routinely delivers public talks, you may upload your slide decks to Slideshare.net and then connect your account to their Facebook app.

If your firm is on Twitter, you may utilize applications to add a Twitter stream tab to your website.

There are additional apps for picture services like Flickr, video services like YouTube, polling services like Poll Daddy, calendar publishing software, and dozens of more tools to help you configure your Site.

Notifications as well as your blog

While modifying your account, go to Edit Account, then Settings, and then to the Notes tab if you wish to make notes or drag your RSS feed onto your business's website.

If your company does not already have a blog, I recommend that you establish one right soon. Second, you may import any additional RSS feeds from your company's website, such as a Corporate News section.

Events

Configure the Events tab – If your business offers events, webinars, meetings, or any other online or offline event, you should establish a Facebook event so that your Facebook page is identified as the organizer.

This enables Facebook users to register for the event and post it on their news feeds, therefore spreading the word about it. If you use an online registration service such as Eventbrite (eventbrite.com). This enables you to create a Facebook Event straight from Eventbrite, saving you time from copying the data.

What's next for your business? You've decided to build a Facebook page, spent some time personalizing it, and then published it. Unless you're Justin Timberlake, Beyonce, or the newest teen band of the year, not even the world's largest companies and most famous personalities can be discovered on Facebook just because they've published their Page. This raises the issue, "How can I entice people to visit my page?"

Create an easy-to-remember URL that redirects to your Facebook page as one of the first things you should do. Facebook will provide you with a bespoke URL, commonly known as a "vanity URL," thus the URL will be http:/facebook.com/YourBrand. But first, you must get the support of 25 people. Most people's first 25 are made up of their coworkers, friends, and family. You may either establish a URL that is a subdomain of your website, such as http:/ facebook.mysite.com (which you customized to connect to the FB page), or you can use a URL shortening service to build a personalized abbreviated URL, such as http:/ bit.ly/brandfb. The next step is to promote your Facebook page. You have numerous possibilities for moving forward.

Twitter

Begin tweeting about your Facebook account. Don't bother your Twitter followers, but let them know that they may also communicate with you on Facebook a couple of days a week. This will assist to improve the quantity of traffic to your Page.

Email Marketing

If your business sends out email marketing, such as emails, business alerts, or anything else, each email campaign should contain a call to action urging consumers to connect with you on your Facebook page. When you initially launch your Website, you will announce it in an article in your newsletter and invite people to like it. Following that, include that information in a static sidebar or the signature part of your email creative.

The company's website

You may emphasize the many social networks in which you are engaged, such as your Facebook page, just like you do with email marketing. This may be achieved by including a separate tab and/or toolbar button on all website pages where tourists can connect

If you want to bring even more attention to your Facebook Page, you should include a Like Box. People will be able to like your Facebook page right from your website or blog, as well as discover who else is a fan of your Facebook page and interact with it via the Like Box.

Marketing on Facebook

You will run customized Facebook advertisements with a link in the appropriate sidebar part of Facebook user profiles urging them to like your article, such as "Facebook Advertising: How and Why You Should Use It." However, understanding that buying a Facebook ad to promote your Page is a low-cost strategy to get your Page in front of a selected set of Facebook users is adequate.

Google AdWords

You may draw followers to the Site using Google AdWords in the same manner that you would with a Facebook ad. Include a call to action encouraging them to like your Facebook page. You may provide a unique gift, organize a contest, or do anything else to peak the customer's attention.

Various Facebook Page Marketing Ideas

There are a plethora of alternative methods for promoting your Facebook Page. They may also be marketed via television commercials, newspaper or magazine advertisements, or other conventional means of advertising. Everything hinges on how a firm promotes, sells, and interacts with its consumers and clients. Finally, strive to promote your Facebook Page in your marketing and advertising campaigns wherever it makes sense. You may promote your website or other contact information in the same manner. Many people chuckle when grocery shops include Facebook logos in their circulars - there's no means to access it and no URL — but it's still a terrific way to show that your firm is current, and some consumers will go home to hunt for Facebook.

Facebook Pages are designed to assist companies, celebrities, and other prominent personalities in establishing a presence and connecting with their fans, opportunities, or customers in general. However, there are instances when you want a private place in which to service a small group of clients or just a distinct spot for your personnel. This is where Facebook Groups come in.

A Facebook group is described as "a real-life link or network with people and things... you're building a community of individuals and acquaintances to support, connect, and discuss pertinent subjects."

When someone publishes or comments in the group, everyone in the group is alerted through email or "red alert warning."

Such emails may look spammy to new members, so make sure to inform them that they may turn off email alerts if they do not want to receive them.

There is now a chat option accessible just to Group members.

You may provide an email address to the Group so that individuals can publish by email while they are on the road. It should be emphasized, however, that those who have the Facebook mobile app may also access groups directly from these applications. Email postings may be aggravating since individuals typically keep their prior email in their email signature and reply data. Once you've established an email address for a Group, you can't get rid of it.

The group configuration choices are restricted.

Choose a group name and a picture.

Select the degree of privacy that is most important to you.

Simply create a description and you're done!

You may also wish to produce a Report to explain group procedures.

Which is more effective: a Facebook Group or a Facebook Page?

You're probably irritated after reading this chapter and trying to find out how to effectively advertise your company on Facebook so you can start connecting with your customers, buyers, employees, and supporters. The functioning of both Pages and Groups on Facebook offers various benefits. Which should I choose, and why?

In general, whether you're a company, organization, celebrity, politician, or other prominent person wishing to communicate with prospects, customers, or followers, you should set up a Facebook profile. The pages are accessible to the general audience.

That is, you may look at all of the characteristics of the Page without being a fan of it. Everyone is welcome to join your Page and express their support in their News Feed.

This is not due to Facebook's agreement to ignore groups. Facebook Pages was developed to encourage companies, celebrities, and other famous personalities to build public Facebook presence. As a result, Facebook decided in March 2009 to revamp Pages to have the same appearance, feel, and functionality as personal profiles. In contrast to your business website, Facebook expects this to be a separate page for your label. Those who choose to embrace it may reap the benefits.

A brand is, for all intents and purposes, the same as a person on Facebook. Search engines may access Pages since they are public.

Groups may be secret, and unless a buddy asks you first, you must ask to join one. If a brand does not have the resources to build a community at the corporate level, a Group might be a wonderful way for them to establish a private community. A Group is also excellent for organizations who want to deliver a quick, private community or a select group of clients to their staff.

Although you should be careful about providing sensitive info on Facebook since you don't know who may see it, it is a convenient method to create a private group. You may form a group that enables you to choose customers for feedback and to explore a possible product or sale, or you can provide particular persons direct access inside the firm. If you decide to form a Group, it is a quick and easy method to interact with your staff.

Chapter 3:

FACEBOOK ADVERTISING

You'll be able to view them anytime you check in to Facebook. When you visit your profile, a Facebook page, or a Facebook group, adverts appear in the right sidebar. Have you ever considered how they should get there? How do they always know personal information about you, such as your age or name? Or how come your friends' names get up on some of the advertisements? Do you want to know how to make an advertisement?

Hello and welcome to Facebook Ads.

Facebook has a wealth of options, some of which you may not see implemented into your marketing campaign, but Facebook Advertising is one of the most basic and extensively utilized platforms to include in your campaign marketing.

In many aspects, Facebook's advertising platform is equivalent to, if not more successful than, Google AdWords. If you're acquainted with the self-service site for Google AdWords, you'll be able to grasp Facebook Ads in no time.

The difference between Facebook advertisements and Google AdWords is that you may customize your campaigns using all of the information stated in the introduction.

Remember all of the personal information you provided to Facebook when you set up your account? Based on their data, you may target adverts to other people.

This chapter covers frequent grounds for denial, a step-by-step ad development procedure, ad performance measurement, and innovative methods to leverage the advertising platform.

Advertising may be rejected for a variety of reasons.

Before we get into the procedures you need to do to create a Facebook ad, consider the most typical reasons your ad may be refused. If you avoid using any of these strategies, your ad should pass with flying colours.

According to Facebook, the top 12 causes for ad rejection are as follows:

- Capitalization of each word—Capitalization of each word might provide you an unfair edge over the advertisements that display. It is, nevertheless, incorrect grammar.

- 2. Capitalizing Complete Terms—One of the easiest methods to shout "SPAM" to your target audience is to capitalize whole words. We've all seen such advertisements, and terms like LEARN HOW TO IMPROVE YOUR SALARY put most people off. Even if the message is beneficial, capitalizing each word makes it look spammy.

- 3. Grammar mistakes—Do you a favor and use good grammar. If you do not utilize good language and spelling, you and your organization will be seen as unqualified.

The only exception is if you are well-versed in vocabulary or grammar and it is suitable for the intended audience. Take your time before submitting your ad for approval to Facebook.

- Incorrect ad language - Facebook is likely to reject ads that do not properly mention the name of the business, product, or offer.

- Deceptive bargains and offers — This should go under the area of "don't be foolish," but regrettably, some individuals attempt to trick clients by promoting one deal that draws them and then giving them something entirely different when they click on it. This will result in Facebook rejecting your ad and perhaps harming your online reputation.

- Images that is irrelevant or unacceptably offensive. Make use of photos that are pertinent to your advertisement. Make certain that your photographs are similarly clean. Don't be a fool, and avoid fraudulent bargains. Contribute to making Facebook a more secure and fun environment for people to engage.

They may be disappointed as well since Facebook has tightened down on the use of frivolous, scantily dressed women in adverts.

- Inappropriate targeting – Why waste money targeting one group while interacting with another? Bottom line: tailor your ad to the individuals you want to reach.

- Destination—Facebook has created some precise standards for directing your audience. Facebook claims that: "When a person clicks on an advertisement, they must be sent to the same landing page. False closing behaviour and pop-ups are not permitted. Advertisements may only be directed to a website or iTunes. The wording will make this evident when connecting to iTunes. Ads may not link to other software resources such as PDF, PowerPoint, or Word."

- Sentence structure—Don't be concerned about using whole sentences. Proper language, spelling, and sentence structure will give your ad, and therefore your firm, a professional appearance.

- Unacceptable use of language—Words in any form cannot be disparaging, derogative, insulting, vulgar, or profane.

- Incorrect punctuation—As in other areas, incorrect punctuation may make the firm look unprofessional. Make care to proofread the adverts for analysis before submitting them to Facebook.
- Symbols and numbers rather than words – The 140-character sublanguage of communicating has changed the way many individuals formulate a statement. Many individuals now use the number "4" for complete words such as "for." This is the reason for Facebook's reluctance. Don't substitute symbols or numbers for words.

Step-by-Step Ad Creation Instructions

One of the finest features of Facebook Advertisements is the ability to test a few Facebook marketing ads in a short time. You may check whatever amount of money you feel like playing with since you pick how much you want to invest.

Designing and releasing your ad is a straightforward procedure now that you've chosen to try your hand at running an ad. Only four steps are necessary for your ad to appear for your demographic target.

1. Design the advertising

When you sign in to Facebook, you may access the advertising area by clicking the Advertising link at the bottom of your screen (you may need to navigate again if Facebook gives you additional newsfeed postings) or by putting http:/facebook.com/advertisement into the URL bar of your browser. Select the Create an Ad option from the ad platform to enter the ad editor. Your advertising is prepared in the first part. Choose the URL that will be the ad's terminus. You may either direct your ad to an external website or landing page, or a Facebook page, party, or program. Choose a name, body content (up to 135 characters), and, if desired, upload a file.

Whether you use cost per impression (CPM) or cost per click (CPC), your ad must be structured in such a manner that it optimizes the promotional budget to meet the aim of moving the customer to a website or creating a brand recognition. Your Facebook ad's design may have a major influence on its efficacy. You should also ensure that the ad is suited to your target demographic. You will focus your efforts on that target audience using the tools offered in Facebook Ads.

Try not to use too many words in your ad's title and body content. Because you don't have much time to maintain your audience's attention, make it focused, brief, short, and to the point. If you want viewers to do anything, such as click on the ad to go to an internal or external website, you must have a clear call to action and make sure your advertising directs them to complete the activity, such as "Click here to register." Photos allow you to communicate directly with people's limbic systems (the seat of emotions). Photos aid in capturing the public's attention and conveying the message. You can't run an ad without an image, so use it wisely. Make use of your company's emblem, a product image, or any relevant graphic. The maximum picture size for Facebook Ads is 110 pixels wide by 80 pixels in height. (Hint: It's not that big.)

If you want to create an ad that displays one of your Facebook page posts, pick Sponsored Page Post under Story Form and then choose which of your recent posts to display, or just let the ad display the most recent postings. If you choose the first option, the ad must automatically update every time you publish a new blog article (and go through the approval process)

Tip

If you can convince consumers to stop what they're doing and interact with you online, make sure you route them to the most crucial landing page. That may be a personal Facebook page, or it could be a community or forum. If you are driving your visitors to another website, consider developing a separate Facebook Ad landing page.

2. Determine your target audience.

Determine who you want to measure with your advertisement. Facebook offers 11 distinct filters, including geography, age, gender, race, keywords, and school.

Take the time to examine who you want to target and how the filters will assist to restrict the ad to that particular demographic as you go through these numerous filters. One of the finest elements of the Facebook Ad network, along with Google AdWords, is this. Take advantage of this feature and apply the necessary filters. To begin, if you only serve customers in the Northeast, you need to set up some filters. Do not just leave the location available to anybody in the United States.

Tip

Using "exact value" targeting may be a highly efficient means of tailoring the ad to the size of the possible audience. Because some of the other targeting choices may not restrict your search as much as you would want or need, this may help narrow it down. If you need to widen a certain interest to a bigger but still relevant audience, Facebook offers topic targeting (topic targets are denoted by a number sign).

Facebook predicts the amount of Facebook people your ad will reach when you specify various targeting parameters. To begin, Facebook forecasts that if you run an ad targeting 22-27-year-old college graduates in Massachusetts, the ad would reach 509,420 individuals.

The smaller the population you approach, the more criteria you choose. Resist the impulse to keep your targeting wide initially to reach more of Facebook's millions of users. Customers must be carefully selected. Even if fewer individuals see your ad, you'll almost likely have a greater conversion rate since you reached your demographic aim.

One possible problem with targeting is that it is dependent on the fields that you and others fill out.

As a consequence, if your location is not visible, or if you have moved and have not updated your location, the ad estimation approach may be wrong. Nonetheless, Facebook has grown incredibly clever when it comes to app placements. Even if you don't share your location, Facebook utilizes your IP address to estimate your location and then displays advertising based on that assumption.

3. **Design an ad campaign and establish a price.**

   You'll need to establish the campaign and select your price once you've developed the ad and chosen who you want to promote to.

You may specify a daily budget and pick whether you want the ad to run constantly or solely between certain dates and hours on Facebook. This may be highly beneficial depending on why the ad is being aired. You must determine what you want to pay for, as well as how much money you want to spend each day and how long you want the ad to run.

On Facebook, you can select between paying for 1,000 ad impressions (CPM) or paying for each ad click. You must establish the maximum offer since both possibilities are contingent on what others provide for the same aims.

Facebook provides a range of bids based on the various proposals it presently has. If you do not provide the maximum amount, Facebook may warn you that it is just the entry charge.

If you're seeking to attract visitors to an internal or external website and your success is contingent on clicks, CPC may be the way to go. You pay per click, so you only pay for each click made by a user. You then must put up your internal or external landing page appropriately to spark their attention and convert them, depending on the conversion notion. If you want to utilize Facebook Ads for promotion and exposure but don't require as many clicks as possible, you may use CPM since what matters is that your ad is seen by as many people as possible. However, keep in mind that Facebook gets money on clicks, and ads that do not obtain clicks will vanish quicker.

Whatever choice you select, CPC or CPM, try both to see how they convert for you. To do so, create a CPC version in one campaign, then click Create a Similar Ad, change the new ad to a CPM offer, and save it in a different campaign.

4. Proofread and submit

After your ad has been prepared, you must now evaluate it. When you're happy with the ad, click Place Your Order to have Facebook look it over.

Advertisers and marketers are usually so preoccupied with the process that they lose sight of the customer experience. Take a tour as a consumer from the ad to the landing page to ensure a positive user experience. Request that colleagues, friends, or spouses go through the processes with you and provide feedback.

Following the submission of the ad to Facebook, it is submitted to a quality assessment to verify that it fulfils Facebook's quality criteria. When your ad is approved, it will be published using the targeting and price choices you specified during the ad creation process.

Facebook gives extensive analytics on your campaign's performance. Utilize the analytics. Don't forget anything. Dive in and see how the plan works. Remove the analytics and make the required modifications to guarantee that your money is spent correctly to get information.

Assessing the Effectiveness of Your Ad Facebook offers an outstanding reporting tool for analysing ad campaign effectiveness. It is vital to analyse outcomes so that you may make modifications not only after but also throughout the campaign. You can make rapid modifications by watching your outcomes in real-time or near real-time, which may radically turn around a slow campaign that is merely draining your financial account.

When you begin a campaign, you are met with a dashboard that gives you a rapid snapshot of the campaign's performance. From here, you may change your campaign, role, regular budget, or timeframe. In addition, you may obtain a summary report of your campaign's key performance metrics, which includes the following:

- Active, Paused, or Deactivated Status
- Reach—The number of individuals who viewed the advertisement during this time.
- Frequency—The number of times each individual viewed the advertising on average.
- Social Reach—the number of individuals who saw that one of their friends was already interested in what you were promoting.

If you provide CPM, determining your cost per click may be tricky. To view the CPM and CPC for each ad, just click Full Report. That is the genuine price. Viewing CPM costs while you provide CPC may be perplexing and useless, but viewing CPM costs when you offer CPM is illuminating. You may also view how much money was spent on each ad within that time. Observing responses can also assist you in determining whether one of your advertising is not being shown effectively.

Facebook also provides three different sorts of campaign reports:

- Advertising Performance

This report provides the same data as the dashboard, but you can modify the reporting settings and export the data to Excel or a CSV file.

- Respondent by Demographics

This report includes demographic data that will help you determine who is clicking on your adverts. This allows you to alter your objectives, automate email, or examine who is attracted to your advertising. Based on reporting criteria, this data may now be evaluated and transmitted.

- Impression Time Conversions

 This report indicates the number of conversions categorized by the length of time between the user's view or click on the ad and the conversion, sorted by the Facebook print time to which the conversion is ascribed (i.e., 024 hours, 17 days, 828 days).

Using Facebook's three reports and main dashboard, you can monitor and change your ads on the go, making greater use of your investment and reaching your target demographic more efficiently.

What are the benefits and drawbacks of using Facebook ads?

Although it may look straightforward to comprehend why or how you want to use Facebook Ads in your marketing plan, there are various options.

Let's have a look at a couple of them:

- New product launches
- Webinars - Hiring - Branding and public awareness - Event marketing

- Social change campaigns

While they all employ the same fundamental ingredients, the outcomes might differ depending on your purpose. If any of these ideas relate to your market, you may test them out to see what appears to connect with your target audience. As you can see, Facebook Ads offers a plethora of uses that may supplement your current online marketing approach.

Like other Facebook applications, the advertising platform will expand with new features and enhanced analytics. Until then, consider this a primer to navigating and experimenting with the Facebook Ads platform. Consider CPC vs. CPM, A/B test similar-goal advertising, modify target audiences, and monitor all of your practices.

When utilized appropriately, Facebook Ads can be a strong tool that provides a considerable benefit to any organization.

Using Facebook Page Analytics to Monitor Your Success

What is the effectiveness of your Facebook marketing and communication efforts? How many of your followers are interested in what you're posting? What causes certain postings to be more popular than others? What can you do to make the situation better?

Facebook offers an abundance of information and insights into the success of your Page and postings. You will understand what your followers are listening to and not doing, what is keeping you from gaining further input, and how to adjust by studying this. Internet marketers have realized that leveraging analytics is vital to success over the past decade, and Facebook marketing is no exception.

Measure and enhance the performance of your page.

Online marketing is a vast subject that covers social media, search marketing, email marketing, and other platforms. You may or may not have been introduced to the notion of Web analytics, depending on your history. Analytics is a discipline that aims to quantify outcomes. It is necessary for every marketing strategy if you want to generate better outcomes and stay competitive in a constantly changing industry. Even if all you want to do is connect with your followers, analytics data can help you fine-tune your message, themes, and approach to keep your audience interested and engaged.

As a Facebook Page administrator, the first stats you'll notice are impressions and feedback rates. These will display just above the date and time of the article on each of the links.

This data will not be accessible immediately; it may take up to 24 hours. The number of impressions represents the number of times the article has been viewed. The feedback rating is based on the overall number of interactions, split by likes and comments.

Insights into Facebook Pages

If you have a Facebook Page, you can view Insights, which provides rather thorough data. Go to your Page and then click the View Insights option in the rightmost column. By clicking it, you will be sent to Facebook's most recent changes.

The Page summary is the first thing you'll notice. Every page includes a description of your User and Interaction. For some unexplained reason, Facebook Insights displays a lot of contact information under Users but not so much under Interactions.

The information in the overview is for the last 30 days, however, you may adjust the date range if you desire.

New likes are the number of individuals that liked your page (become fans) during that time. There's also an up/down indication that shows the percentage change from the prior time.

Lifetime Likes is the total amount of likes you have received during your life.

Monthly Active Users, including nonfans, are the number of Facebook users who have engaged with or updated your Site's post content. When compared to the preceding period, this statistic likewise indicates a percentage trend.

In the first table, Participating Users are further separated into eras. It goes to reason that fewer individuals will visit or engage with your website on a single day than they would over a week or month.

Even additional information can be found in the Interactions section: - Post Views show the number of times a post has been read in NewsFeeds. This figure is substantially larger than your total number of followers since fans will see many postings.

- Post Feedback refers to the number of likes and comments on your News Feed. This statistic is lower than the Monthly Active Users figure since web views are not included.

Let's go a little further and look at some additional information and maps by clicking on the Users link in the left menu (under Site Overview).

Facebook Page Insights' Users section

There are six more info graphics and a wealth of stats on the User's page.

The chart for Active Users is the same as the one on the Overview Page.

Daily Active Users — this graph depicts the interactions with postings for each day. Unchecking the Post Viewer box is a good idea since that number is typically significantly greater than the others, making the variation between the other metrics difficult to observe.

Post likes exceed post comments in this case, which is true of most sites. It is also usual for there to be more likes than unique page visits. Your followers will see posts in their News Feed far more often than they will on your real Page. This review page has a larger percentage of Pageviews than the norm.

New Likes and Sources of Likes - This graph shows how many new individuals like your article on the page each day.

The graph represents the usual weekly cycle utilized by most online analytics companies – users act differently on various days but consistently each week.

When you see a decrease in new followers, as in this example, you may want to investigate new and more direct sales techniques, such as Facebook advertisements.

A selection of those fans' favorite sources may be found next to the New Likes table.

Some sources remain unclear since Facebook is not always able to trace them all.

Demographics — Facebook Page Insights offers two pieces of numerical data: an age and gender map and the lists below.

A gender and age chart may be useful in many situations. Check to see whether this demography fits any other information you know about your target audience.

If not, you may need to approach other cases more efficiently using Facebook advertisements, or the information from other sources may be wrong. Because Facebook gathers a vast quantity of information that users willingly share, this demographic information is extremely likely to be true.

The lists of nations, cities, and languages may be enlarged to reveal more, although not all of them will be visible. To determine penetration rates, divide the number of fans in each city by the total population. Do you need to focus more on cities? To broaden your reach, create some advertising that targets individuals in those cities.

Page Views — this graph displays the number of people who visit the Facebook page regularly. According to PageLever, just one to six percent of followers check your Facebook profile daily (published on AllFacebook.com). The remainder is looking at your content as they navigate through their News Feeds.

You can view the proportion of people that visited your site, including the Wall and other tabs, below the map. Because of the low amount of Page visitors and even fewer trips to custom tabs, I propose that your key Facebook marketing techniques be advertising and posting.

Custom tabs are beneficial, but they have a limited influence.

Search engines are another key source of referrals. Webmail domains and sub-domains may show in this chart when you send users from your marketing emails to your Facebook page.

This map measures how much time followers spend shooting photographs, viewing videos, and listening to music. It is logged here when users click on your videos, photographs, or music. This might be beneficial if you're curious about the effectiveness of your various sorts of postings.

When we turn to the Interactions tab, the first map, Daily story feedback, looks just like its counterpart on the overview Site, except it now contains Unsubscribes. Unsubscribe occurs when viewers hit the down arrow on stories in their News Feed that are linked with your profile, rather than when they opt to delete the links.

In this scenario, if you have more unsubscribes than views, and the bulk of your articles have reaction rates of less than 0.5 percent, your postings are unlikely to connect with your audience.

I recommend aiming for a feedback rate of 1.0 percent on your postings. The feedback figures show how consumers discovered the goods they liked. Even if you don't reach a high proportion of your followers (impressions divided by user count), compelling content and calls to action like "Press Like If..." or "Tell us in the comments below..." may help you achieve a 1.0 percent or higher engagement threshold.

Use Web Analytics to determine the Facebook Effect.

Most companies want to discover what their Facebook followers desire on their main website and what activities do not work. Do fans buy things? Are they as engaged in the web site's content as those who discovered it through search engines? What can we do to persuade more Facebook followers to make a purchase or do another specified activity on the website?

My advice is to make certain that your system aids you in testing:

- What kind of postings do your website's diverse followers wish to see?
- How do particular Facebook ad viewers interact with your website?

With this information, you may modify your approach to obtain more of the intended impacts on your website.

Chapter 4:

THE INFLUENCE OF LOCALS: FACEBOOK SPACES AND SALES

There have been many ways for promoting local companies and franchisees in the context of web marketing: Before the Internet, shops depended on phone book advertising, local TV commercials, periodicals, and the bulk of what was known as mainstream marketing. Craigslist launched a large-scale growth of its online ads in the year 2000.

Search marketing marketers (AdWords, Yahoo!, and comparable PPC providers) could target their advertising to particular localities from 1998 to 2002.

In 2005, Google Maps (formerly known as Google Local) was integrated into Google Search. Local businesses started to show in search results in 2006. They are instead strongly mixed in with search results depending on the search query.

Along with Living Social and BuyWithMe, Groupon, which was created in 2008, is the most well-known local daily aggregator.

In 2010, Facebook introduced Spaces, then in 2011, it introduced Deals.

Nonetheless, local online advertising is a multibillion-dollar industry:

According to Google, the potential for local advertising in 2012 is $16 billion.

Check-in offerings on Facebook are entering the broad market to benefit millions of little companies.

Facebook transactions started in early 2011 in Canada and Europe, followed by Australia and South Africa in August 2011 and Israel in September 2011.

How does Groupon compare to Facebook check-in deals?

Facebook originally tried a daily deal offering in many locations before abandoning the experiment in August 2011. Despite its massive network, Facebook has determined that the approach is unsustainable. Similarly, it has to be seen if the Groupon platform will be profitable. In comparison to Facebook's transition away from daily promotions and toward check-in deals provided by particular companies, we may be comparing apples to oranges here. But first, let's take a look at the two primary actors in local marketing.

Groupon-like enterprises are considered to hold the greatest influence via their email list—this is how they offer tiny businesses to customers. Groupon has more than 115 million users, and hundreds of salespeople contact companies regularly. However, Groupon, like other businesses that follow this strategy, must continue to promote and call. This adds a lot of overhead. Facebook already has 706 million active users, providing it with an unequalled network for gaining access to and selling firms to consumers–all at no extra expense to Facebook.

Facebook offers several benefits versus Groupon, including:

Because Facebook has a social interaction network, many of which are local, check-in offerings are crucial. Groupon sends email inboxes based on the deal; most are worthless to the vast majority of email subscribers, and there is no social proof or confidence in them.

In the future, Facebook Credits might be tied to Check-in Deals, enabling Facebook or local marketing businesses to attract users to do so in return for a discount or free credit.

Under Groupon's concept, businesses must give substantial discounts, which diminishes profitability and might lose them money. The promise of customer lifetime value may be false since bargain hunters who only purchase at huge discounts may go on to the next deal with no commitment to your firm. Facebook can provide more targeted offers with reasonable discounts, allowing companies to benefit while screening out unscrupulous bargain hunters.

What are Facebook Places, exactly?

Check-in Deals and their other location-tagging applications are built on Places. Users may share their vacation locations and submit images from prior journeys on Facebook.

Facebook introduced the ability to tag practically anything, including photographs, status updates, videos, and a location, in August 2011. Places may be utilized as business locations, and you can claim or construct your own on Facebook. You will have additional options to advertise and expand your company if you create or manage a Facebook Place. If prospective consumers can visit your company, they will tell their friends about it—this is free word-of-mouth promotion for you!

There are a plethora of creative ways to utilize Facebook Places. To begin, MasterCard collaborated with Facebook Places to distribute 20 seats from the former Yankee Stadium around New York City. Customers may win Yankees tickets by scanning a QR code located on each seat.

Facebook currently provides location information for practically everything on the network:

People will tag their images with the displayed location.

If users are publishing while traveling, they should provide their current location.

As Facebook's location capabilities expanded, places would ultimately blur into a variety of sorts of location information that users would associate with practically all Facebook postings.

You may enable the What Tags Function in your privacy settings. You may also activate Profile Check to allow any posts that include your name before they are uploaded to your profile. When you receive the new Timeline, you become more conscious of your profile as a reflection of your life and values, and you won't want to be included in that representation with all of your affiliations.

How Facebook Places Function

Mobile Users of Facebook may check in to a Spot to see which of their friends are nearby, as well as identify local locations and deals. If a certain retail business provides a Checkin Deal, users may observe indications about it as they travel about their subway area (assuming the retailer tells consumers).

When users check-in (by phone or desktop computer), an alert may display on their Facebook, in the News Feeds of their friends, and on the Place tab. When logging in, users have the option of adding their friends. Users may now assign a particular location to images, videos, and other Facebook material.

By clicking the Sharing button, users may share places with their friends. The pop-up window enables people to connect with a restricted number of friends on Facebook, a relative's Wall, a group to which they belong, or in a private message.

How to Make a Facebook Page for Your Company

First, determine whether your company already has a Facebook Place. If you can't locate it, it's probably not yet a Facebook Place. Please remember that location pages are not the same as Facebook pages or Community Pages.

True Place pages include a map of the area, a list of friends who have checked in, and a stream of activity from prior check-in pals. To complicate things further, you may link the two by having Facebook understand that both pertain to the same item when you designate your firm as a

Location, presuming you already have a Facebook Page for it.

How to Construct a Location

Sign in with a Facebook app on a smartphone or other web-enabled device at that site to establish a position, if Facebook Places are accessible. Then, go to Locations and sign in using your Facebook app. You'll be asked about your current location. There is also a synopsis of the location and tag mates. Then, once again, hit the Login button.

When you return to Facebook, search for the Position and add it as a company if it's yours.

Companies with Multiple Locations

When your organization has several locations, Facebook organizes everything utilizing a parent-child connection. The parent page is the main page of the firm, while child pages are place pages for individual branches or locations. Store managers and franchisees may be expected to monitor and edit these children's sites for firms with hundreds of locations.

It is crucial to highlight that, for the time being, creating a parent-child connection between pages requires the aid of a Facebook official.

This sort of one-on-one assistance is only offered to companies with substantial Facebook advertising expenditures. However, public features for smaller multi-location enterprises are expected to be offered in the future.

Facebook Check-in Deals

Facebook Deals are digital promos that are accessible online, and they are currently free to produce. As a business owner, this enables you to motivate consumers to come in when they shop, boost the awareness of your brand among their friends, improve store returns, and develop loyalty. Because of Facebook's social feature, the business may become a part of customer and friend relationships. Most companies are unclear on how to obtain more visibility and followers after initially joining Facebook. While many organizations utilize Facebook advertisements to increase their visibility and followers, others do not have the resources. Deals on Facebook are one way to bridge the gap.

What is the most effective method for finding Facebook deals?

You may locate offers by using a Facebook app on your smartphone. A yellow ticket may be used to highlight nearby sales places.

Many companies might profit from Checkin Offer posters on Facebook. Deals are typically discovered by Facebook users when their friends post them, when companies advertise them, or when they visit https:/www.facebook.com / Checkin / Deals. You may check in at a retailer to get a discount.

What kinds of check-in specials may you offer?

Check-in Deals are offered in four varieties:

Personal Deal – You may sell a one-time deal to current or new customers.

Friend Contract — A deal in which numerous people must check in at the same time. This service is available for parties of up to eight persons.

Loyalty Bargain – A deal that needs a specified number of check-ins (between 2 and 20) per customer to be claimed before it may be claimed.

Charity Bargain A deal where your client donates to charity.

What steps should I take to build a Facebook deal?

There is a link at the bottom of the Deals page, or you may go straight to http:/www.facebook.com/deals/business/. To begin, click Contact Us and complete the contact form. A Facebook team member will contact you to help you with the finalization of the transaction. There is currently no self-service option for constructing deals.

Here are a few things to remember while negotiating a contract:

To urge customers to act, offer at least a 10%–20% discount or provide a gift with a purchase that is worth more than the item bought. You may offer higher discounts, such as 50% off, but keep the margin in mind. Facebook Deals provides benefits over Groupon that don't entail handing up the farm.

Keep the contract as straightforward as possible in terms of timing and location. Customers that are unable to grasp your offer quickly are unlikely to take advantage of it. That is not due to people being ignorant; rather, it is because most people are extremely busy and preoccupied. The hooks are straightforward and enticing.

Request that your personnel stock the ready-to-redeem offerings. Ensure that everyone is up to date. If you run your discounts for a lengthy amount of time, people may grow bored and may stop checking back on them. They'll presume you'll never update them.

Also, don't run too many promotions at once; when clients have too many alternatives, they don't pick any of them. If you have too many identical discounts, customers may feel dissatisfied and give up on the distinctions.

Deal Concepts

Only one's imagination limits one's ability to sell. Here are a few ideas to get you started:

Unoccupied rooms at a hotel with a massage may be offered incentives. Are your guest shop revenues down recently, but you've got a huge audience this weekend? What about conducting a one-hour discount sale with a 20 percent discount? Alternatively, if you manage a hotel that mostly caters to business visitors but has a new feature or offer, establish a deal to raise awareness of it and encourage clients to check it out. Is there an excess of certain food in the kitchen?

Make specific Room Service arrangements. Of course, quick transaction development and implementation demand structure and worker control, since they may have to occur at inconvenient times when not all management is accessible.

Casinos and resorts target guests who have already checked in with a range of promos. Other casinos and resorts may provide specials for massages, entertainment, and food discounts.

In Australia, a bank gave out free movie tickets to everybody who established a new account.

How do you get your firm ready for a transaction?

Planning and preparation are necessary to launch, advertise, and support a deal.

Here are a few things to consider:

Ensure that your staff is aware of the contract and that they are accurate. So, what's the story? Is there a limit on the number of redemptions? Can the same customer utilize the offer more than once? When is the offer going to expire? How will staff maintain track of the bargains that have been redeemed if clients redeem the deal by revealing the screen of their phone to employees?

Do you tell both applicants if the contract is no longer valid, or do you keep it? If you have hundreds of locations, make sure you convey everything to the store owners and provide them with your mobile phone number. Make yourself accessible to answer any questions you may have until you have all of the necessary information.

Customers should be informed about everything that surrounds it. Is there a hand-out or a signed paper with all of the information, obligations, and terms?

Ensure that you have adequate stock on hand to fulfil demand. Do you have enough employees to cope with traffic and service customers?

Check that the logos, images, and postings on your Place account are in excellent shape.

Think about running Facebook ads. Summarize the offer in your commercial and send it to the Site, Location, or tab that explains the transaction.

So, haggle with all of the purchasers and profit from the sale!

Chapter 5:

SOCIALIZE YOUR WEBSITE AND BUSINESS WITH FACEBOOK CONNECT AND SOCIAL PLUGINS

When we speak about Facebook, we tend to concentrate on the different ways you may utilize it. Facebook recognizes that the more value it gives, the more often you'll come, the longer you'll stay, and the more others you'll tell about how fantastic it is. Facebook has spent considerable time establishing a set of services aimed to attract you to become a part of its company. It's a powerful engagement loop.

However, Facebook is also working to extend its influence to the rest of the Web, expanding the circle of interaction to encompass every platform on the Internet.

Because they boost your capacity to engage with new prospects, existing customers, and brand followers, Facebook's social plugins, which extend Facebook to the rest of the web, provide you with additional chances as a marketer.

Facebook Connect is much more than a blue "Connect with Facebook" button that allows you to check-in using your Facebook credentials instead of registering for the site. According to Facebook, Facebook Connect is "a powerful collection of developer-friendly APIs that allows people to transport their identity and relationships everywhere." Facebook Connect is a sophisticated tool with a plethora of functions that can be implemented into websites.

Integrating Facebook Connect enables marketers to draw more visitors to your page, enabling you to connect and sell additional chances while also integrating specialized applications inside Facebook Link. It also provides additional resources to users who visit your website and removes the need for users to form a new login merely to leave a remark or connect with your website in another manner.

Remember that the website that employs these social plugins does not get any of the information that users supply - it all goes to Facebook, where users see a customized experience based on Facebook's social network (the relationship between you and friends).

Among the social plugins are the following:

Users may share their websites with their Facebook friends by using the Like button.

Users may share their posts with their friends by clicking the Send button.

Feedback— Allow users to enable a comment function for Facebook users on their website.

Event Tracker – Inform people on their website about what their friends are up to.

Suggestions – Make customized suggestions to users.

Let's start with an overview of how all of these plugins will interact with your website. You must copy and paste the code onto your website in each situation. That means you'll need a basic grasp of HTML as well as experience modifying templates. There are just a few lines of code, but you must know where to place them.

In certain circumstances, there are even easier options—for example, if your website is based on the WordPress platform, you may be able to locate a custom-made WordPress plugin for the Facebook social plugin. If your head is racing after reading this text, it is preferable to transfer such duties to your web developer.

Some of the benefits of utilizing Facebook Connect and its social plugins are as follows:

Users who are already signed in to Facebook may join your site with a single click, validating their accounts using their Facebook credentials.

Socializing – This feature enhances the social, customized, and familiar aspects of your website. Show new visitors that their trustworthy friends already like your website. Users who are connected to your site may see, comment on, or evaluate what their friends have viewed on your site. As a consequence of social evidence, trust is swiftly formed.

Maintain relevancy – Because social networking has grown in popularity, your website may look out of date and boring without it. People enjoy the emotional, familiar experience to which they have become used in recent years, with the addition of a social component.

Incorporating a "Like" button on your website

It's worth noting that the Like button has taken the position of what used to be known as the Sharing button. Have you ever noticed how rapidly things on Facebook change?

The Like button enables users to share your website with others. When someone likes your page, a story with a link back to your website shows in the user's News Feed. Furthermore, if you provide information about your website when generating the Like button, it may appear in the Likes and Interests area of your friend's profile, your website may show in Facebook search, and advertisers may target individuals who like your website.

When you use Facebook's helpful wizard to create the Like button, you can also add a Send button.

If you want to show the number of Likes in your button, remember that this statistic includes more than just the number of individuals who clicked the button; it also includes shares, likes, and comments on posts about the URL, as well as the number of private Inbox messages containing the URL.

When you're finished, hit Get code to get the code you'll need to incorporate into your website.

Some of the most socially progressive websites, such as Yelp, enable you to post tales in your stream. When you rate a restaurant on Yelp, you may use that review and business information to update your Wall. As the Like Button may be used to share a website or blog piece, this story sharing capability automatically sends material to your Facebook Wall while you engage on other websites. This is beneficial for websites that can utilize it since the stream tale frequently contains part of the website's branding, such as a logo, leading to enhanced brand exposure.

Timeline.

Several websites now employ this social interface to enable you to share your Facebook activity. This option is often seen in social networks and games that encourage users to share information to make their resources more visible.

Facebook links a live feed to your peers about what you like by referring to the many sites you like hanging out on the internet. You may be scared that if too many people see your status updates, they may begin to cover them up or unfriend you.

Don't worry, the news feeds of your pals will only show you what they're up to. Everything they overlook perishes without making a move against them.

Using the Distribute button, you may send your website to particular friends, Facebook groups, and email addresses. Because you must enter each contact's or email address, the Like button frequently reaches more of their friends than the Send button.

This may be found at

facebook marketing for beginners.docx

The Like Box social plugin helps you get more followers and consumers from your website by using your current fan base. Have you ever worked in a restaurant or bar with a big queue of customers waiting outside? We declare, "It must be in an excellent place! We should go as well!" This is an example of social testimony inside an organization. If you're not aware of social proof, it's the premise that when people see how many people like you or your business, they're more willing to set aside their scepticism and give you a chance. The first regarded you favourably.

In the Like box, you have many alternatives. The simplest method is to just show the number of individuals who have liked your page, along with their faces. You can, however, screen a selection of recent posts if you prefer.

This is one of our favourite social plugins, although it is not suitable for all users. The first thing you should ask yourself (and as many other people as possible) is if your fan base looks to be remarkable. Sure, not every page needs 10,000 or 100,000 fans — in fact, for a small specialized company; a few thousand may be enough.

If you feel the number is too low, it shows that displaying off may result in social disproof rather than social facts. "Why aren't they more well-known? They're probably not that good!"

Including Facebook Comments on Your Website, One of the most typical Facebook Connect connections is commenting. This feature enables users to opt in to submit comments on a blog or website using their Facebook account credentials (assuming they aren't locked out of Facebook, which most people are until they sign out purposefully).

Many forums and commenting services, like Mashable.com, have incorporated Facebook

Connect into their systems, making it simple for blog and comment program users to add Facebook Connect to their sites. This has resulted in more Facebook Connect involvement for voting reasons. More than one-third of new authors have originated through Twitter, according to The Huffington Post, one of the world's most popular blogs.

If you have a WordPress account, you can use a plugin.

Disqus is free online feedback and discussion software utilized by CNN, Newsweek, Fox News, and Engadget, among others.

Facebook Comments networking plugin is available at facebook marketing for beginners.docx

Using the Live Stream feature to include conversation

The Live Stream feature enables customers to speak side by side while watching either streaming or static content on your website. Users sign in to their Facebook accounts and utilize the status update tool to continue discussions.

The Live Stream was initially utilized during Barack Obama's presidential inauguration, and it helped Uber become well-known.

During the inauguration, CNN.com aired the festivities live and offer you to communicate with your friends who were also watching on CNN.com through Facebook Connect.

Nobody could have guessed how many people would go to CNN.com and start conversing with their pals about this once-in-a-lifetime encounter.

CNN had over 136 million page views, according to Mashable.com.

CNN.com received over 600,000 Facebook status posts.

During the show, CNN.com transmitted almost 4,000 status updates to Facebook each minute.

CNN.com received 8,500 status updates during President Obama's inauguration address.

Because of this tremendous success, additional event organizers have turned to Facebook to enable event-related interactions. The NBA All-Star Game, the Michael Jackson Memorial, and a live watching party for Bravo's "Real Housewives of New York City" finale have all utilized the Live Feed.

We may see even bigger events use the Facebook Live Stream into their platforms in the future.

Consider watching the Olympics, attending a concert, seeing the World Series, or viewing a movie while conversing LIVE with all of your friends who are experiencing the same thing.

The Live Stream elicits emotion and links us to something with which we may be able to identify. It brings us together with our friends for a significant occasion. The network thinks that by including this feature, we will spend more time on their website, and Facebook will assure that we use their app more often. Unlike Facebook activity hash tags, it also allows the majority of your network to see your status updates, the question about what you're up to, and finally, join in on the fun.

Using Facebook as a registration and login method for your website

The notion of single sign-in has continued to proliferate on the Internet as consumers have become more annoyed with the various websites they must sign up for to access information. Open ID, for example, has sought to provide a single sign-in that consumers can use across all of their websites. When Facebook Connect was released, 400 million individuals were able to utilize a single sign-in method immediately away.

As users rely increasingly on social media, Facebook often gains from becoming a single sign-on platform. Because you can use Facebook to sign in to all of your favourite websites, you are more inclined to connect with it.

Another benefit of utilizing Facebook Connect as a single sign-in method is that when you log in to Facebook or connect to any website using Facebook Connect, Facebook automatically logs you into all of the websites you connect to. This assures that if you visit five locations that utilize Facebook Connect, you will not have to input your login credentials more than once. Furthermore, when you log out of one account, Facebook may log you out of all platforms. If you're using a public computer, this may save you from having to sign in and out of every website you visit during a surfing session.

Registration may become one of the most popular elements of Facebook Connect as the company grows.

The setup of the database is the easiest portion. It has a code, much like other social plugins. When the programmer takes over, taking the information from user signups and translating it into the website, things become more challenging.

You may build a customized experience by using Facebook Connect.

We just got a glimpse of Facebook Connects capacity to tailor the experience. Some of the information you've provided on Facebook, such as your age, gender, location, or content, may be used by Facebook Connect to help develop a narrative about you alone. You can go as far as your imagination will allow, and your programmers will assist you in getting there.

To fully grasp what creating a personalized Facebook Connect experience includes, it's essential to learn about how some users have opted to utilize this feature.

The Discovery Channel explored methods to persuade people to watch the exclusive programming during Shark Week 2009. The Discovery Channel determined that one method would be to grow into neighbourhoods where people already gather. Instead of watching Shark Week advertising on the Discovery Route, Chapman and his team at Campfire (previously known as the Advance Guard) opted to utilize Twitter as a digital channel to locate new consumers.

The most straightforward option would be to utilize a Facebook ad with a call to action. So, what if you could persuade people that they are on a shark-infested boat?

What if you could make their heartbeat seem to be genuine to them? Wouldn't that be amazing? Frenzied Waters, a shark-themed app, utilizes Facebook Connect to develop a shark-themed app during Shark Week. By using data you had previously made public to Facebook, such as biographical information and images, the Frenzied Waters program created an atmosphere that made you feel as if you were a part of the shark attack.

The 2011 Museum of Me

(facebook marketing for beginners.docx from Intel was unanimously recognized as one of the greatest instances of Facebook Connect personalization to date. When you connect, you'll be transported through a creative museum that features your photographs, phrases, videos, and friends. A Friendship Museum may be more successful in investigating your ties with them.

These two applications generate empathy and transport you to another universe.

This tends to hook you up and make you want to rush about and share it with your friends because it's so great. This form of word-of-mouth marketing is the greatest that any company or product could ask for.

Not only for the internet.

Although the bulk of this chapter's attention has been on brand websites and pages, some of Facebook Connect's applications are still accessible on the iPhone. Facebook Connect is becoming more popular, especially among applications that give ratings of entertainment and eating alternatives such as movies, music, restaurants, pubs, and hotels.

Flixster, a popular software for film sharing and ratings, has incorporated Facebook Connect, allowing you to check how your Facebook friends evaluate a film. Urban Spoon, another popular iPhone app, currently has approximately 6,000 active users each day.

The importance of this, although amazing, is not in the statistics. UrbanSpoon relies on Facebook users as reputable sources. Referrals from friends are more trusted than any other source. This is the secret sauce used by applications like Flixster and UrbanSpoon that utilize Facebook Connect.

We need to figure out how to sort through all of that information in a world where we are assaulted with an average of 35 GB of data every day. One method is to do precisely what we would do in our offline lives: seek information from friends, family, and coworkers. Instead of reading what the New York Times food reviewer thinks about a local Italian restaurant, you can now utilize UrbanSpoon to see what your friends, family, or colleagues think about it. Was the Parmigiana Chicken tasty? Is it easy to locate a parking space? Worst Customer Service You've Ever Seen? Your Facebook friends will instantly inform you. The app's incentive is that you will keep coming back since it gives helpful and trustworthy information. Why would you not return to Flixster when you can see movie trailers, discover the closest movie theater and showtimes, and hear what your friends think of the summer's anticipated hit?

Summary

As shown by the examples in this chapter, Facebook Connect and its social plugins are excellent tools for integrating into your website, blog, or application. It has been regularly shown to enhance traffic and engagement. The beautiful thing about Facebook Connect is that you can choose from a variety of connectivity options.

You may start by introducing content sharing on your website right away, while you work on methods to incorporate social filtering into your application and deliver a tailored experience for your users.

One of the most exciting features of Facebook Connect is the social graph of your website, website, or organization. You can determine who interacts with your website based on the information Facebook has on each user. You may use such data to develop content, offers, and demographically tailored alternatives. Facebook is likely to embrace Facebook Connect expansion to provide more options and versatility.

Chapter 6:

USING FACEBOOK TO DEVELOP COMMUNITIES

People are building communities based on their hobbies, events, companies, goods, services, celebrities, schools, and even their favourite cuisine! We establish and engage in these online communities in the same way that we do in the real world. We interact, connect, exchange articles, submit photos and videos, and ask others who share our interests to join us. Simultaneously, some old-school blogs are assuming the role of new communication methods.

Some businesses choose to create these autonomous communities using platforms such as Jive and Lithium. These enterprise-level communities provide more features and flexibility, but they are also more costly and best suited to bigger enterprises and organizations.

You will also have to work harder to lure people to the party since these premium communities are hosted on a separate domain or a sub-domain of your website.

On the other hand, Facebook makes it simple and inexpensive to form communities. Facebook is an ocean where community builders may fish for individuals who have similar interests or hobbies.

One benefit of utilizing Facebook to form communities is that it provides broader scope by breaking down geographical restrictions. Some traditional communities are becoming big enough to split into local chapters and community organizations throughout the globe. The division into regional groupings is not feasible on Facebook unless people elect to do so. Instead, no matter where they are, they may all engage and benefit from one another.

When creating your group, you must decide who will be your Community Manager. In an ideal world, you or someone on your team would be that person.

As the community manager, you must provide reasons for individuals to return to your community.

Nowadays, we all have far too many challenges competing for our attention. Those that capture our attention and are significant, helpful, valuable, or otherwise required should remain in the limelight. Furthermore, you must include your community to maintain an engaged and expanding community on Facebook; yet, you cannot engage them just by altering your profile or group status every day. You must present content in a variety of forms since each member of your group will demand a different method of accessing their facts and expertise. Some of us enjoy the video, while others prefer images, and yet others may prefer links to thought-provoking articles.

Let's look at some of the many sorts of communities that may be built on Facebook, how people interact with them, and some recommendations to help you get the most out of your community engagement. In this section, we will discuss many types of communities:

Customer Communities are built around companies, products, and services.

Private business groups for internal discussion

Private networking and business communities

The remainder of this chapter will look at ways to increase involvement and engagement in Facebook groups.

Creating a Community for Your Business, Product, or Service

Because more and more of your prospects and customers are on Facebook, it should not be overlooked as a viable tool to establish a community. Even if you've built a private company network, make sure your brand is correctly represented on Facebook. Facebook might potentially be a source of new community members for your private community, whether via a Facebook page, Facebook marketing, or both.

Creating an active Facebook community around your business, product, or service may be useful, particularly if you are successful in promoting conversions. Why is Facebook so effective at engaging users? First, when a community member likes or comments on one of your posts, Facebook may tell the person's friends and is more likely to highlight that engagement in the News Feeds of other followers.

You keep the business front of mind if you communicate with customers, purchasers, and followers frequently. Combine it with daily advertising and the addition of fresh content on Facebook and other websites, as well as the improvement of the brand's name.

Create a stronger community via pages or groups?

We discussed the distinctions between Pages and Groups before. Pages, as previously said, give more possibilities for marketing and analytics, while Groups provide more options for notification and privacy. Neither one creates more culture per se, but here's what each one excels at:

Pages — After becoming fans, many seldom return to the original Page. Fans will see updates from your Page but not from other fans on the Internet.

If users do not like or comment on the postings, they will no longer view them. As a consequence, the conversation must be steered and energized. Request feedback and likes.

Groups — Because everyone in a Group is alerted when another member Group writes or comments, individuals often return. You don't have to do the same to keep folks interested. The members assist in keeping people interested.

Those who don't want so much activity will quit the group, therefore they'll never reach as high in membership as Pages. As a result, they are ideal for your consumer segments who are particularly passionate about certain themes.

What impact does your community have on your ROI?

In-depth community or engagement talks may often bring up dormant worries regarding ROI in social media. The best approach to answer is that community development does the following:

- Increases brand recognition via fan buddies
- Increases fans' and buyers' trust in your brand
- Customer loyalty to your brand is increased.
- Reduces the cost of client acquisition
- All of these items may help your company's earnings.
- Constructing Private Corporate Communities

Using Groups, Facebook allows you to create private communities. This is ideal for businesses with dispersed employees or a growing staff that want their team to hang out and interact in a shared location. Large organizations often have private enterprise communities established for them on a professional community platform.

Companies that don't require a lot of features or don't have the cash for a premium platform, on the other hand, may use Facebook to fill that communication hole.

Many businesses have discovered that their staff are all on Facebook and spend a significant amount of time communicating on the network. Instead of requiring people to log in to another website, they opt to utilize Facebook as an internal messaging tool for their group.

One disadvantage of utilizing Facebook instead of a private community is that you do not have control over the data, even if the group is private. As a result, be careful when disclosing anything private or confidential. You don't monitor the data and aren't privy to Facebook's decisions about the site, and you wouldn't want to wake up one day to discover that, even though it's impossible, Facebook has decided to make groups fully accessible, exposing confidential data that could be detrimental to your company and beneficial to your competitor. If you meet those criteria, you should consider one of the numerous private corporate group networks or a private network like Yammer.

Making Use of Facebook as a Focus Group

Continuing with the idea of utilizing Facebook as your company's private community, how about starting a Facebook Group to serve as a private focus group for your business, product, or service?

You may invite certain prospects or customers to this Facebook Group and use it as a platform to communicate with them.

Demonstrations and exclusive access should be provided.

Display images of impending items or software releases.

Solicit honest feedback.

You may not want to display something that you are concerned may be revealed. However, if you have any form of blogger or PR connection, you always face the danger of displaying early versions of a product or software—and leaks aren't necessarily bad, are they? They may occasionally feel the buzz and build client expectations in the same way that a new film trailer does.

Constructing Social Networking Communities

Facebook allows us to create our social networks. Such communities are springing up all around us. Most of the time, such particular communities arise on the user's profile; however, when these communities get large enough, the user must establish a page to prevent Facebook from putting suitable constraints. These communities may sometimes evolve to be bigger and more powerful than a typical organization. How is this possible? The social web, as Chris Brogan and Julien Smith put it, enables us to become "trust agents." Trust agents, according to Brogan and Smith, are "digitally savvy individuals who use the web to humanize companies via openness, honesty, and real connections." As a result, they have enough online power to make or ruin a company's reputation. Be of Assistance

One of the simplest ways to begin developing a solid community is to be as helpful as possible. Be a resource for the community. As a result of your ongoing help to your followers, they will begin to approach you with issues. Because of your resourcefulness, your community may begin to suggest you to others, allowing your community to become larger and closer. Make Use of Lists

Using the Facebook List function, you can establish little communities for yourself based on hobbies, geography, school, job, or whatever else you want to construct a list around. While this will not help you develop a community in the sense that you are bringing others into a private area where you are interacting, it will allow you to connect with members of your community regularly. Setting up lists and checking in with those lists regularly might assist to make an expanding personal network more manageable. It may also assist you in organizing your community around your various life segments.

List ideas include school, employment, hobbies, and geographic area.

This may help you segment your information sharing, which is particularly useful if you have a diverse set of likes. For starters, you may be a gourmet who enjoys sharing recipes, reading intriguing articles, discussing TV food programs, and leaving status updates about the many places you frequent. You may decide that this information is not of interest to the persons with whom you engage.

You will ensure that you only share the material with those people of your circle who are foodies by putting them in your circle.

Even if they are unaware that you have developed a gourmet list, they will enjoy the focused content for your foodie group. (At the moment, people on your list are not told that you have added them to the list.) Although all of these strategies may assist you in growing a community, developing relevant contacts, and increasing your impact and reputation, you must ensure that everything you do is authentic. Please do not be dishonest while attempting to establish a community.

Don't do it for the numbers or the imagined authority you'll get. It erodes people's trust and does not bode well for developing a community around a hobby or interest for both customer communities and personal networks. Building a community around a pastime or a specific interest might sometimes be more efficient for both customer communities and personal networks. There have been specialty communities for many years. Many of us spent time on a discussion board conducting research or participating in a dispute that was of interest to us.

These themes may include a passion for automobiles, music, fitness, a city, or just about anything else you can think of. Individuals continue to belong to many organizations in their personal and professional life; hence, online communities serve as excellent places for them to keep involved with others.

Is your company involved in any of these activities, or do you provide goods and services?

If so, you may join other Facebook groups that have already been formed, or you could start your Page or Group to develop a community. Instead of constructing it around your product or service, it may be created around the activity or pleasure your company, product, or service provides. This community would not be used just to advertise your business, product, or service, but rather to have discussions about the industry in which your firm operates.

Increasing Facebook ad community participation

While large corporations may already have millions of followers and may not need to employ Facebook advertisements, small and medium-sized businesses may struggle to create a large enough group.

In the early days of Facebook, it was quite easy to get a large number of free followers; however, this is no longer the case. Facebook has disabled several tools that allowed for free fan growth, and Page owners are becoming warier of what they see as spam advertising other Pages and Groups. Facebook advertising fills this need and may be used inexpensively to build a sizable fan following or community.

Even pages with millions of admirers may desire to launch a new group or page for one reason: invisibility to current fans. Facebook's EdgeRank algorithm decides which followers see your Page's postings.

Fans who haven't loved or commented on articles for a long time no longer receive updates on your community page. According to one survey, just 2.79 percent of their admirers watched posts with moreover a million fans daily. That indicates they didn't have millions of people to reach; they merely had tens of thousands. The result is that fans and members provide you with a chance to keep people engaged, and you lose them if you fail to do so.

How to Find Low-Cost Fans and Group Members There are two basic approaches to reach prospective community members using Facebook Ads:

Use the targeting options available on the Facebook ad creation page.

With the headline and ad text, you may target a certain audience.

The cheapest clicks are frequently obtained by targeting no-brainer specific interests. If your company offers cooking-related things, for example, target cooking or the name of a famous cooking program.

If you can't acquire those tailored advertising for less than $1.00 per button, keep the targeting options open and reach out to the masses in your headline. In the United States, for example, you may target everyone with a headline that asks, "Do you like cooking?" This will only be chosen by your prospective admirers, and since the targeting is so wide, the price is minimal, as is the cost per click.

How to Increase Interaction in Your Community

Offer Exclusives Is there anything you can share with your community on Facebook that hasn't already been shared elsewhere?

This is especially crucial if you communicate with some of those same individuals in other online communities such as Twitter, MySpace, LinkedIn, or a private social network.

If you have a medium to a large community, try to introduce a new product, a technological upgrade, or corporate news on Facebook first. If your community discovers that you are likely to provide information about the firm through Facebook, it will check in regularly and become an active member of the community.

Instead of continuously sending films to YouTube or uploading videos from other video providers, why not create such videos right on Facebook?

Submit any new product ideas and share them exclusively on Facebook first. Leave them there for roughly a week before uploading them to other picture providers. Tell them exactly what they want.

These are just a few examples of areas where you may develop various types of content and keep your audience engaged. The most crucial component of keeping your community involved around your brand, product, or service is determining what your community wants and needs from spending their valuable time on your Facebook page or group.

This might be your vision to present. Instead, deliver that degree of involvement and information type to the community on a regular and continuous basis.

Check in with your fans regularly to determine whether you're getting what they want. When you do decide to experiment, measure the interaction to determine success. Examine the levels of reaction for each article and its experiences. Is it on the rise? If this is the case, you are increasing your visibility and engagement.

Community development

You need to start cultivating your community now that you've decided what kind of community you want to establish, whether it's a Facebook page, group, or both, and you've spent some time modifying the settings and building it up. What should you be doing? Just provide some status updates now and then? Isn't it a little monotonous? That seems to be one of the most often asked questions by these companies since establishing a Facebook page or group. Comprehensible. Experiment with a couple of the following observations.

Organize Competitions

Running tournaments that are exclusively available to your Facebook group is a proven method to get your customers interested. The simplest and fastest approach to do this is to look for answers to specific questions or topics of conversation. You may sell your online business, as well as a free month of operation, a voucher, and other items. It should be noted that Facebook's rules of service require you to conduct competitions via an app, and Wildfire is the most well-known platform of this kind.

Always Participate

Getting your Facebook audience engaged is one of the finest measures you can do. Don't squander all of your effort building this beautiful network just to have it concentrate on collecting automated updates from RSS feeds, YouTube, or Flickr applications. Come hang out in the neighbourhood. Change your ranking once or twice a day. Use a status update to inquire about the audience's day or their thoughts on a certain problem. Make a few remarks back to those who take the time out of their busy day to communicate with you. Again, this is easy, yet it is often overlooked and forgotten. Simply being there puts you far ahead of many other firms, including maybe your competitor.

These are just a handful of the numerous ways you may remain involved in your community. In truth, civilizations have no control over themselves. We need someone to keep prodding them with interactivity, engaging talks, and various types of information. The more you can do this with your followers, the more of a nurturing, flourishing, engaged community you will have on Facebook. This is especially important if you opt to create a Facebook page rather than a group since all of your participation will be visible to everyone, not just community members.

As we begin to discuss all of this interaction, I can sense some trepidation forming. I understand your concerns. You are concerned that someone may write anything nasty about you on your Wall. You're worried that you'll be insulted, mocked, or spit on for one reason or another. You want to find out how to accomplish it.

How do you tell whether you're doing a good job?

1. Examine the first 5 to 10 postings on the page.
2. Count the number of likes and comments on each one and average the total.
3. Is this amount roughly 1/100 of the total number of fans (1.0 percent)? If that's the case, they're doing a fantastic job.

On the other hand, the Coca-Cola Page has 33 million admirers but only roughly 10,000 likes and comments every post. That equates to just 3/10th of its total fan base.

This implies that Pepsi is only viewed by a subset of the 33 million fans. We've seen enormous sites like that still obtain 0.1 percent–0.3 percent response rates, implying that Coke will only be available to 1 million to 5 million followers. That's still a lot of people, but not quite as many as you may have guessed when you saw the 33 million figure. And the upshot is that if a competitor page with 10 million followers performs better in terms of interaction, it may be more visible to Facebook users than Coke is.

The only way to win with Edge Rank is to collect more likes and comments on each article.

You may have realized by now that this commitment might be time demanding! Even a small firm must spend at least fifteen minutes every day on social media. And the more ambitious your aspirations for your community or social media, the more likely it is to become a full-time job. Fortune 500 companies may have an entire social media team.

Is it your responsibility to keep an eye on your Community?

The issue of negative comments is one that every brand that creates a Facebook page must address. While this may be an issue for Groups, particularly those with contentious topics, you may be more concerned about Facebook Pages because comments and content are always public. But keep in mind that because few people go back to the actual Pages and because fans in their News Feeds don't receive Pages posts from other fans, only the biggest brands are vulnerable here. I

If you're a big business with hundreds of millions of users, certain people probably have had a bad experience with your business. Although only good things would be openly spoken about by others in an ideal world, this is certainly not the case. What you don't know will do you no good. Exactly right? Incorrect. Such discussions take place 24 hours a day and are vital to your ability to find them and react.

Okay, let's say someone shares something offensive on your Wall — what are you doing? Simple, huh? Just remove it and proceed. You only want the good and entertaining stuff on your page.

There'll be people, online and offline, who for one reason or another are not happy with your brand, product, or service. They will leave the comments online inside your various online posts, like your Facebook page or group. If the comment isn't violent, excessively disruptive, or continuous, leave it alone. You then have to decide whether to reply to the comment.

Both decisions have both positive and negative consequences. If you do respond, on the one hand, it could spark a never-ending back and forth that could add fuel to a smoldering fire that would otherwise have put itself out. On the other side of the coin, though, if you don't respond, you appear to be ignoring the person or the complaint that the person is bringing to your attention. This might have an adverse effect as well. The best advice is to judge on a case-by-case basis every comment. Others you're going to respond to, while you're going to decide it's best to leave them alone for others.

Facebook and social media tracking

You need to track any comments regarding your management, company, industry, or competitors. Make sure that what you are writing suits your PR plans and social media practices before you respond.

However, consider that the response could be better until you agree to reply. Don't let people who try to threaten you trap themselves, and never react if you're emotionally disturbed by the emotions of a consumer.

Facebook Pages themselves provide group administrators with some degree of warning, and other free resources are available, such as HyperAlerts (www.hyperalerts.no) (www.hyperalerts.no). There are plenty of professional-grade tools available, including Radian6 (www.radian6.com) (www.radian6.com). We suggest you set up a listening and monitoring tool, like Radian6. Just keep in mind that monitoring social media can be complicated, and you can keep track of dozens of metrics there. Make sure that the tool you choose can provide insight into activity in your space with the data you need.

Chapter 7:

ADVANCED FACEBOOK MARKETING STRATEGIES

⬚ Affiliate Promotion

Affiliate marketing is one of the most successful and entertaining methods to earn money online since it requires a lot of experimentation on your side, particularly when you first start figuring out what kind of affiliate offers to perform on your affiliate sites.

What excellent affiliates like most about affiliate marketing are the concept that by selling products, they can earn a lot of money without having to do anything. Merchants will give you things to advertise, while affiliate networks will provide logistics and ad units, allowing you to employ your chosen marketing method.

The great majority of affiliates market their affiliate offers via websites, which remains the most popular affiliate channel and is publicly endorsed by the majority of affiliate networks to this day. Many affiliates, including video streaming services and social networks, market their affiliate offerings via alternate channels.

Because Facebook is the world's biggest social network, users go there in the hopes of breaking it high.

Finding a single affiliate who has succeeded in making Facebook a profitable platform for selling affiliate items, on the other hand, is difficult since you can't advertise affiliate sales on Facebook in the same way you can on a website.

▪ Begin by disseminating high-quality content.

If you use Facebook to coldly pitch affiliate bargains, you risk failing miserably as an affiliate marketer since Facebook users can detect affiliate marketer postings a mile away and have learned to disregard them.

In truth, the Facebook algorithm is excellent at keeping sales-related postings outside of the news feed to maintain a decent user experience. You will concentrate on creating high-quality content that provides value to leads.

The simplest method to provide value to leads is to share material that might assist them to answer queries about the sort of items you offer and then swiftly connect links to your partner after one or two beneficial updates!

◻ Promote Your Affiliate Offers Using Groups and Pages

Now I can't encourage you to perform affiliate marketing on Facebook from your profile since you risk being reported as a spammer. Create sites and communities that promote your company as an affiliate instead.

Groups work especially well since they are often seen as communities, and the individuals who join will value the material that you promote there. The ideal technique is to form a group centered on a very popular market, then begin posting your material first and then connect with your affiliate afterward!

Do not be afraid to post connections to your partner in groups other than your own, but be conscious of where and when you do so. Exchanging affiliate links, for example, is often beneficial around the holidays, as well as in deal-focused groups.

☑ Reduce the length of affiliate links

Facebook has strict anti-spam policies in place, as well as content URL limitations. At the absolute least, a badly positioned referral link will reduce the value of the content, and at worst, you will be flagged. Shortening product URLs is the simplest technique to prevent bans or irrelevance.

Keep in mind that not all contact shortening services are affiliate friendly, therefore I recommend utilizing "tinyurl.com" to shorten your affiliate links.

☑ Make use of images in affiliate postings.

Ones with images always convert exponentially better than posts with text. Focus on a single product illustration or a clean backdrop and text graphic when selling a product. Remove gleaming images since they are automatically categorized as spam.

◻ Post product evaluations on Facebook using video.

Were you aware that the Facebook algorithm lends a lot of weight to Facebook video posts? That's right, by creating a Facebook live video to market your stuff, you may receive a lot of hits and purchases, plus people adore review videos!

First, use Facebook Sidebar Ads to redirect leads to a landing page. Facebook dislikes it when marketers use Facebook advertising to push partner sales, but there is a solution! Simply create sidebar adverts to attract customers who are lovers of the business or products you promote.

Now, neither Facebook nor partner networks appreciate it when you send leads directly from an ad to a product page, so take your time to create an interesting landing page for visitors to go to when they click on your Facebook advertising!

How to Significantly Increase the ROI of Facebook Remarketing ROI or Return on Investment, is critical for any marketing effort to be successful.

If a firm or corporation is to achieve a net profit, its savings must surpass its profits.

Remarketing is one of the most effective techniques to avoid this.

What is the definition of remarketing?

As the name implies, remarketing is a straightforward idea. It is a strategy of promoting and selling items to clients from whom you have previously bought.

This may be performed by gaining access to email lists, contact lists, or any other folder on or near your website.

Once you've established a tailored following on Facebook, remarketing is a fantastic tactic.

What exactly is a custom audience?

A bespoke audience is similar to a target audience in that it is a particular demographic of individuals who are more likely to engage with your business. It is not limited to persons of a certain age or gender; it might be as wide as "those who read a lot of books."

If you're a bookshop, you don't want to target folks who haven't read a bestseller since high school.

Creating a one-of-a-kind audience Facebook, like the Facebook Advertising app, has its viewer creator.

You may begin by opening a Facebook Ads account. If you already have one, you are welcome to continue.

Begin by visiting the Facebook website's custom audience page, or by visiting the Facebook Advertising page and selecting the "Audiences" option in the page corner.

Uploading Customer Data: When you reach the user's production page, you will be greeted with a brief popup that will let you upload a file containing customer data.

Don't worry if you don't have an organized list of client emails or ID numbers; Facebook has you covered. You may submit a variety of attributes to the viewer creator to seek customers on Facebook.

Some examples include, but are not limited to:

▢ Phone Number for City, State/Province

▢ Year of Birth Date of Birth

▢ Gender Age

▢ First Name Last Name

▢ Zip

▢ Gender

▢ Age

▢ Postal Address

Once you've submitted a file containing one or more of these pieces of information, you may name the audience for future reference.

The first step in creating a focused group is deciding what you want to be on the lookout for. Three buttons may be found at the top of the Custom Audience tab:

— Create a Saved Audience — Create a Lookalike Audience — Create a Custom Audience

You'll almost always need to utilize a stored crowd if you've previously gone through the process of building a custom audience. Examine the first two pushbuttons.

The first one, titled "Building a Custom Audience," is undoubtedly the first page you arrive at. It is preferable to create a Lookalike crowd after you have previously created a Custom Audience on which to base it.

Make a unique audience.

After choosing 'Building a bespoke audience,' you will be led to the same pop-up page you saw after picking one of four generic list styles: Traffic in general / Internet traffic / Mobile operation / Facebook interaction Once you've decided to create one of these lists, you'll be able to add names or other information to create a bespoke audience.

Create a Lookalike Audience

If you already have a stored custom audience or a Facebook page with some traffic, you can quickly construct a lookalike audience based on individuals who have shown interest in your brand.

Choose the Facebook page where you want to base your audience. Choose a general area from the search box and a population range of 1 to 10% of that location's population to base the audience on.

You may create up to six lookalike audiences for a particular area, so make use of various places around your country during your ad campaign.

Using the Facebook Search Bar for Market Research On Facebook, it is critical to be aware of what people are interested in and post about a certain subject in a plethora of material and media.

You may believe that learning about the industry is difficult, but it's not with Facebook; it's all about understanding how to search.

Understanding your target market

To do market research, you must have a thorough understanding of your target population. At this stage in the marketing campaign process, you should know a lot about your viewers and the kind of individuals they are.

Having Similar Interests

Assume you're a merchant who specializes in office supplies. An analogous interest-based quest might be something like going to the search box and typing in "posts appreciated by individuals who love fountain pens." This phase requires a lot of critical thinking, but it's a skill that can be learned just like any other.

Examine Related Pages There's nothing wrong with visiting a vendor's Facebook page that also works in your specific specialty. Competition is excellent for a company, and researching other items in depth is a smart method to learn what they're up to. What are their choices? Are these excellent or terrible decisions? What kind of individuals are admirers of the pages?

Analyze the categories

Take a swing when searching for a certain age group or category if your fan base is enormous or has a wide age range. If more than half of your audience is under the age of eighteen, it is time to start thinking about how to better appeal to them.

Keywords

Knowing how to utilize a search engine is an important component of understanding SEO or search engine optimization.

SEO refers to how essential a certain brand or piece of content is to a given search. Because certain keywords will always be more relevant than others, SEO plays a significant role in the branding process.

It is critical to understand which terms are most often searched in your niche and to generate content that will boost your SEO ranking in connection to such keywords.

What do other people think?

Consider this: not everyone who visits your Facebook page will be tempted to join you on your first meeting. A few excursions are required for many consumers to fully engage with your organization.

Nonetheless, many individuals will forget your company's name. Consider how someone would describe your brands in a few words if they couldn't recall the name while performing market research.

Using a search engine with the proper keyword combinations on the main page will not always provide good results. Many Google or Facebook users don't browse beyond the first page, but that doesn't mean you shouldn't.

Perhaps the third or fourth page down is what you're looking for. This is not to say that these bits of information are unimportant. With Facebook algorithms, certain companies or phrases may be put behind others.

Localizing the searches: One challenge is looking up a broad topic. While this is a fantastic starting point, you'll want to limit your inquiries to a certain location. According to recent surveys, more than half of Facebook's mobile searches have a regional focus.

It makes perfect sense. If a customer is seeking a new salon for a haircut, they don't want to obtain results that show businesses hundreds of miles away.

Using keywords that contain the terms "around me" or "in my profession" is one of the most powerful and essential abilities you will learn.

Facebook is also a lucrative destination for all types of developers, particularly those trying to build new applications.

You may also discover how Facebook intends to grow into the app development sector by visiting developers.facebook.com.

What's it like to be a developer on Facebook?

When you create a Facebook Developers page, you may perform a variety of things. Some of these capabilities include the ability to:

⬚ Promote your account organically

⬚ Optimize and monitor consumer behaviour

⬚ Monetize your mobile app or website via adverts

Create a Facebook Messenger platform for your app to increase user engagement. There are easy links to get you started on both Android and iOS products, so there will be no misunderstanding about how to get started as a developer.

How do you create a Facebook developer account?

If you land on the Facebook Developers page, a fast link to get started on Android or IOS will display at the top of the screen. When you click on one of these programs, you will be directed to a sophisticated website that details the numerous sorts of features available via the Facebook Development program.

You may go through all of this if you want, but for the sake of time, let's get straight into the big event and get you registered as a developer.

If you scroll down to the bottom of the page, you'll see something like a green button. It will say "Fast Start" on it. Go ahead and click here to start the account creation process.

A pop-up window will then appear, requesting that you agree to the account's Terms of Service. As usual, it is recommended that if you have the chance, you take a quick look and go over some crucial points. Accepting the Terms of Service will get you one step closer to the next download.

You'll next be prompted to give the display a name. After that, you'll need to prove that you're not a Captcha machine, but don't worry, it's not difficult.

The Primary Menu

The developer's home page design will provide you many menu alternatives to pick from, including Preferences for Dashboard Near the Settings Alerts for Roles close Nearby User Analysis Most of these will be meaningless to you until you've previously constructed a user, so for the time being, focus on the process of actually producing an item.

Making an app

The first step is to determine the name of the app. After entering a name, you must complete another Captcha before proceeding to the application.

After then, choose one of the four platforms that have been provided to you. You will be able to upload your SDK from there (you will need to download the App building tools) and upload it to the interface.

From there, you may add more SDKs to your device, supply the app with metadata, and any user events you want to offer, and you'll be finished with the rapid setup.

Facebook Developers Can Benefit From These Guidelines

While cooperating on Facebook app development, keep some of these principles and pieces of advice in mind.

• Modifying a visually appealing gadget depending on the framework you employ. If you're making a cross-platform app, you won't want it to appear the same on an iPhone as it does on an Android.

Understand your target platforms; understand the Android and iOS UI application guidelines.

Don't simply make an app because you think it looks cool. Create an app that is aesthetically appealing to the platform you are utilizing. What you believe is desirable may not be appealing when combined in a single system.

Testing, testing, and more testing. The easiest method to iron out bugs on your device is to conduct many tests to ensure that all of the settings, windows, and functionalities function properly. Simply because something worked once does not guarantee that it will function again the next time you open the program.

Chapter 8:

MONETIZING FACEBOOK

Facebook is a wonderful tool for reaching out to consumers by sharing photographs and comments. You may start conversations and get vital consumer feedback. This engagement is how many companies generate money on Facebook in an indirect manner.

Furthermore, Facebook may be a powerful tool for earning direct cash for your product or service. Through Facebook advertising, you will reach hundreds, hundreds of thousands, or even millions of prospective clients.

Making money on Facebook is straightforward, but it will be much more effective if you follow certain best practices.

Selling online, whether via a website, blog, or email newsletter, is quite simple. Simply said, you exhibit your products, promote them to your target clients, and then urge those people to buy. Your customers will pay for your product or service in whichever way they see fit, whether it's delivering a pound of apples to your door in return for 30 minutes of consultancy, billing you through PayPal, or just writing you a check. To increase your online sales, you must go beyond the essentials and understand the art and science of selling online.

The usage of Facebook for online selling is no different than any other strategy.

All you need to do is post your goods or services, wait for payments, and make a livelihood. You may even go a step further and understand how Facebook can significantly enhance your online sales and e-commerce earnings. This chapter discusses how to use Facebook to sell items or services online.

Your corporation will create a business page rather than a corporate or personal profile Site. Use your personal Facebook page as a Business Page instead.

Before you build a Facebook Page for your company, make sure you have a properly configured personal Facebook page. Use a nice picture, fill in all of the information, and carefully study and choose the privacy choices that are most comfortable for you.

Multiple managers are permitted on Business Pages. This is ideal for developing organizations with high turnover — you can be certain that if one administrator quits the company, someone else will be able to handle the Page.

Business pages are made public by default, so they show in search engine results.

To make search results more relevant, company sites are separated into multiple categories, such as brand, local business, or artist.

With a personal profile, you must accept friendship requests. In contrast, anybody may become a fan of your Business Page without the consent of an administrator.

Once you've created your Facebook page, you must keep track of its progress regularly. At the most basic level, performance may be measured by how many people like your Facebook page, how many users are participating, and which articles are shared the most.

All of this can be verified using the analytics tools on your Facebook profile.

To summarize, one of the first stages in selling online is to create a Facebook Page. You will use your Facebook profile to publish information about the items or services you provide. Analytics may help you determine how well your Page is doing, how effective your material is, and what the most significant components are creating. I go further into Facebook statistics (and more broadly), but first I examine Facebook's algorithm.

Facebook's Algorithm

When attempting to boost engagement on Facebook, keep the algorithm used to view posts in mind. A shared post's prominence in a person's News Feed is determined by the Facebook algorithm. Its idea is similar to Google's well-known PageRank algorithm, however, it is used to Facebook rather than Google, and it uses different data.

A search engine algorithm focuses on the fundamental processes and website design, which might vary over time, but the algorithm handles such changes. The PageRank algorithm takes into account the number of reference links to a website, but those connections must be picked up by search engines to be included in its computation (and these reference links may be affected by other variables of a website).

In contrast, the Facebook algorithm is based on human behaviour and the uniqueness of that action. As a result, you mustn't examine just your capacity to monitor Facebook data more often than a web analytics tool, but also the quality of your followers' interactions. The content determines how followers understand your messages, which is crucial if you want them to return to your Page regularly.

Increases in affinity and weight improve your algorithm rating, however, older posts are seen as less significant than fresh entries. Affinity is built on the exchange of likes, messages, links, timeline entries, and comments. The more interactions that occur around certain functions, the more you can influence your algorithm's ranking.

There is no model package or post-interaction combination. There are, however, things you may do to increase your affinity and weight: Encourage people to enjoy your content by asking them directly. Energize your consumers by inviting them to join your List of Fans.

Post photographs, movies, and slideshows with fascinating material to encourage comment and variety from individuals who are affected by sight and sound.

When writing to your blog, instead of utilizing a closing statement, construct your article such that it offers an open-ended question and encourages your followers to interact. The algorithm will clarify the engagement and how it presents the content to a bigger audience.

Determine when your posts are most likely to be seen. Some networking platform applications, such as Crowdbooster, propose timings based on previous postings.

Insights

Whether you take the effort to go through the steps you believe the algorithm will take to enhance your affinity and weight, you'll undoubtedly want to know if it has any impact. This is possible with analytics dashboards such as Facebook Insights.

These dashboards are designed to help you manage your communication activities. The Facebook Insights dashboard displays all Facebook insights linked to the following attributes in a single view: Websites that show and employ Facebook social plug-ins, such as the Like button.

Applications include test apps, mobile devices, and desktop apps.

Facebook pages, both those produced on Facebook.com and those included in the Open Graph protocol, which gives third-party access to Facebook (such as websites and mobile phones).

You may, for example, provide data on particular tales that people appreciated on your website or how many people commented on the articles on your Blog. This data shows you what material is most essential to your audience, allowing you to capitalize on it.

When you visit your Facebook page using the Statistics dashboard, you will see a variety of analytics and traffic information (or users). At the top of the Facebook Insights Page, you may choose one of four pages: Description, Likes, Reach, and Thoughts on This

The Summary section provides a quick snapshot of total likes, friends of friends (how many friends the people who liked your page had), people talking about it (how many people communicated with your page by posting to your Timeline, commenting, or taking other actions), and total weekly reach (how many people saw any content related to your Facebook page).

One of the most essential aspects of the Overview area is that it displays the posts on your Page and contains information such as their reach, number of engaged users, number of users talking about this (talking, commenting, or otherwise interacting with a post), and virality (the percentage of people who have engaged with your post versus someone who has just seen it and not engaged with it).

What I like to do with this portion is filter the posts based on one of the criteria (reach, engage people, speak about this, or virality) and check which posts have earned the highest scores. This is necessary so that you can determine which material was most appealing to your viewers (or valuable). For example, one of my video-containing posts had 342 views, while a couple of other articles received fewer than 200 views. My audience (and most likely yours as well) enjoys watching videos.

When you click on the Likes option in the Facebook Insights dashboard, you'll see the gender and age of the individuals who liked your post, as well as their nations, cities, and languages. You can also see where your preferences come in - from your Timeline, a Like box, or a Like click — from this location.

The meet is the next statistic in Facebook Insights, and it provides stats similar to the Likes tab, but it is tied not just to who likes your Page but also to who you meet. This section also gives information on how people perceive your material. Organic ways (such as who viewed your material in a News Feed), paid (advertising), and viral (someone saw a friend's content or Page) are examples of such tactics. The total impact of all three ways may also be observed.

The last section of the Facebook Insights tool is the Talking About This feature, which displays user-related data from reviews, queries, and other interactions with your Facebook page. This information is only available if more than 30 individuals discuss your website in the last seven days.

You may choose whether to show monthly or weekly results in the top-right corner of the Page.

If you choose monthly data, the dashboard will automatically default to the most recent complete month. When you choose weekly data, the dashboard automatically defaults to the most recent full week. You may also narrow down the date range.

To the top left of the Facebook, Insights Page is a drop-down list with start and finish dates. When you click on this option, a date range list appears, allowing you to input the dates you wish to view (e.g. JANUARY 3, 2020-JANUARY 30, 2020).

If you are confused about the date range you are looking at, you may see the possible possibilities by hovering your mouse cursor over the question mark next to the statistic.

To export the data, go to the dashboard's top-right corner and choose Export data. A dialog box appears, asking you to choose the date range for which you wish to export data, as well as whether you want the data to be viewed as an Excel or CSV file.

Instead of bouncing from tool to tool, Facebook provides additional analytics tools that help social media teams to focus their limited efforts on producing outstanding customer experiences.

Many of them provide the ability to download data into an Excel spread sheet, with communication focused on their analytical capabilities. Remember that, unlike Facebook Insights, these tools do not mainly concentrate on Facebook comparison sources, so their reach may vary significantly from what you are looking for. If you want to understand more about how the Like button affects your Account, Insights could be the best place to start. Others, such as PageLever, provide a more visually appealing package with the same stats.

Each of these analytical methodologies offers evaluation tools to assist guide social media actions, and they also include integration into the Facebook profile. This is vital if you want to compare Twitter activity to Facebook activity, for example. Many of these gadgets have varying costs, however, the majority give either a free preview or a free trial. The next sections go through some of the various analytical equipment.

PRO HOOTSUITE Hootsuite, a Twitter desktop program accessible at www.hootsuite.com, offers a dashboard where you can examine Facebook, Google Statistics, and Twitter analytics.

Hootsuite lets you personalize the appearance and feel of this data from various social networks to reveal as much or as little as you desire. The analytics dashboard is available as part of the sophisticated Hootsuite Pro package upgrade, which has a minimal monthly fee.

CROWDBOOSTER

Crowdbooster (facebook marketing for beginners.docx) is a dashboard analytics application for measuring Twitter conversations. It also puts communication on Facebook sites to the test. The impressions of a message determine commitment in Crowdbooster. Crowdbooster compares the overall number of impressions to the number of likes.

It provides a graphical representation of messages that may have garnered the greatest popularity and responses, enabling you to propose removing messages that have little influence on followers. Crowdbooster also suggests fans remark on your profile, advising you on who you should follow up with to build your affinity and weight. The dashboard is superior to most others, such as Hootsuite, since it lacks a daily data summary and the free version of data downloads. The graphs and information on your fan page might be of instant assistance in taking action.

PAGELEVER

PageLever (facebook marketing for beginners.docx) was founded in 2011 and provides a dashboard for managing several Facebook Pages. It divides its dashboard analytics into three categories: fan metrics, visibility, and interaction. It emphasizes important facts, such as the most sensitive demography of your Sites. It also calculates percentages such as the commission rate and displays a variety of dynamic graphs. This tool adds a lot of intriguing graphs and information to the metrics that display in Facebook Insights.

For example, reference sources show how users arrived on your fan Page.

POSTING

Postling (facebook marketing for beginners.docx) combines several Hootsuite and TweetDeck cross-platform sharing tools and adds overview message delivery to your account, blog post access from inside the user interface, and Twitter user effect measurement.

In terms of Twitter, Postling will overlay visit data and send you an e-mail with an evaluation of your metrics.

This site is better suited to Twitter than Facebook, however, it provides an overview.

Small and medium-sized businesses often utilize Google Analytics (facebook marketing for beginners.docx). As a business intelligence tool, it has assisted websites in understanding their traffic sources and has enabled businesses to adjust their campaigns, whether from search engine optimization, banner advertisements, pay-per-click ads, content marketing, or offline sources. However, there is one distinct impediment to its deployment that has vexed Facebook company owners.

To address this segmentation issue, Google has modified its strategy to better fit the way consumers locate websites online. Google Analytics version five featured a social plug-in function. The tool offers social engagement reports that assess how visitors share information on your site through social activities. These social behaviors include Facebook Like button clicks, Google+1 button clicks, and Delicious bookmarks. The reports compare three forms of social media-related activity: the number of pages viewed each day, on-site average time, bounce rate, and other visit indicators.

These segments distinguish between individuals who have utilized social activities accessible on your site and those who have not.

The number of social actions (+ 1 click, likes, etc.) for each social source and social source–action combination.

A comparison of the number of actions on each page of your site to the information presented by social source or social source–action combination.

The upside for your organization, particularly if a website is its primary digital presence, is the opportunity to identify effective social media channels deserving of more participation and time commitment.

SOCIAL WEBTRENDS

Webtrends is well-known for its enterprise-level web analytics (facebook marketing for beginners.docx).

Webtrends Social, a dashboard tailored to small companies, has been introduced.

Facebook. It provides a social media management platform that enables marketers to execute, manage, and grow social media operations across teams.

You may monitor your Facebook Timeline, develop shared apps, assign replies to team members, and assess your productive efforts on Webtrends Social. The free version only allows for one Page, however, several Pages may be managed for a minimal monthly fee.

Facebook offers a variety of advertising options based on what you want to promote: a page, a case, a Facebook application, or your website. These ad kinds are selected when you initially create your ad and when you choose your ad's destination.

To get started with Facebook advertising, go to facebook marketing for beginners.docxor click the Create an Ad link at the bottom of your Facebook Page. You may choose what you wish to promote from this page. This might be a link to an external website or a Facebook destination ID (such as a Page, app, or event). You may also choose to advertise directly on a Page or Place, or an application or event. In this example, I will choose a Page.

You now have three options: Increase the number of page likes. This enables you to reach a broader audience.

Posts on the Page should be promoted. This allows you to increase the number of people who view and interact with an essential post.

See also Radical Alternatives. Some more advanced advertising solutions, such as cost per click, may be developed.

For the time being, simply concentrate on expanding your present Facebook page to a broader audience.

COST AND BUDGETING DETERMINATION several promotional components must be perfected to ensure that your Facebook advertising is more than simply a lovely symbol on a computer screen and adds to sales. The amount you spend on advertising is significant when calculating the profitability of your advertising campaign. For instance, if you spend $5 per click for an ad and receive 10,000 clicks, your ad will cost $50,000. If you purchased a $10 item from only 100 of those who clicked, your advertising income would be $1,000. For each advertising bundle, you lose $49,000. You must calculate your advertising to determine the optimal price to pay for it to maximize your profit per click.

LIFETIME BUDGET, DAILY SPEND LIMIT, AND DAILY BUDGET

You have complete control over how much money you spend each day. Your daily budget is the advertising budget you select for a new campaign. This is the maximum amount you desire to spend on that advertisement on each day that it is advertised. When your daily budget is depleted, your adverts will immediately cease showing. From your Advertising Manager, you may alter your daily campaign budget or stop or delete your ads at any moment.

When you sign in to Facebook, go to the bottom of the page and click the advertising icon to access Facebook's campaign management. Because some Facebook pages are rather lengthy, I found it a bit difficult to click this button. Another option is to go to www.facebook.com and click the advertising link at the bottom of this page.

It is important to note that your monthly budget differs from your daily spending limit. The daily spending limit is the limit established by Facebook for handling payments, and it grows automatically when you make payments at previous limits successfully. It is analogous to a credit rating.

Impressions available are the number of impressions or views accessible to the advert based on your targeting. The winning offer is the average cost per click you agree to pay, which decides how often the adverts are broadcast. Every day, at midnight in your selected time zone, the cap is reset. When you complete the payments, your daily spending limit will be increased immediately. However, you will never pay more than the amount of your daily maximum budget.

In contrast to your daily budget, your lifetime budget is the total amount of money you're prepared to spend on Facebook throughout your advertising campaign. The total amount you spend on your Facebook ad campaign will not exceed that amount.

You may alter those settings in your Ads Manager once you've made your ad live.

You'll see that the Period is modifiable in your campaign settings. Each ad in a campaign is sent based on those parameters.

In the Facebook Ads Manager, choose the campaign you wish to modify (which is evolving as from this writing). A budget column appears at the top of the page. To adjust the budget or schedule, click the pen symbol next to the dollar amount.

You may adjust the daily budget of your advertising campaign and the lifetime budget of the campaign using the dropdown list below. You may also change the campaign timetable in this section.

THE AUCTION SYSTEM

Facebook advertising uses an auction-based bidding mechanism, which means that the market determines the price of your ad. When you place a maximum bid, you are indicating that you are prepared to spend up to that amount per click or thousand views of your advertising.

Here's how it works: your maximum bid competes with other marketers' bids to determine which advertisements are displayed to the target audience and how much you eventually pay (up to your maximum bid, never reaching your daily budget).

If you're attempting to reach a highly coveted audience during a very busy time of day, you're more likely to have to spend the maximum offer for every click or impression.

Facebook may assist you in determining the appropriate bid amount for your advertising, or you can make your bid selections by selecting the advanced mode (see the Advanced Mode link in the Campaigns, Pricing, and Scheduling section of the advertisement-creation tool).

The recommended range of bids displays the range of bids that are presently winning the auction from advertising similar to yours. A bid price should be placed within or above the price range specified for your ad. The maximum bid is the highest you may spend for a click on your ad or per thousand impressions produced, depending on whether you want to pay per click (CPC) or per thousand impressions (CPM). Facebook only charges you the amount necessary to win the auction for your ad, which may be less than your maximum bid.

After running these adverts for a period, you will begin to refine the text, pictures, and discounts to determine what performs best with each category of clients. You may also begin reaching out and attempting to reach new audiences.

IN FACEBOOK ADVERTISEMENTS, THE LIKE BUTTON

The majority of Facebook advertising has a Like button. Like is a typical Facebook gesture used to attach meaning to various online objects such as photos, timeline posts, status updates, and comments. Users express their emotions about your business or group by clicking Like and then sharing their thoughts with their friends. If users who are interested in your company or organization notice that behaviour in their ad edition, their friends may notice it as well. The Like button appears in your ad only if you are endorsing something on Facebook, such as a website, program, or event.

When you swing your mouse over a Facebook ad, an X appears in the upper right corner of the ad. When you click on this advertising, you have two options: hide the advertisement or hide all adverts linked to this advertisement.

The X is a way for users to provide quick and easy feedback on Facebook advertisements.

Facebook considers this feedback because it improves the advertising program for all advertisers and users.

How to Assess the Effectiveness of Your Advertising

You may measure your Facebook advertisements using several analytics, just like any other kind of advertising.

You may use Facebook to assess how many people your ad has the potential to reach based on your target demographic. You may also examine survey results and the number of individuals who have seen your advertisement for your campaign. This section looks at different methods for gauging your readership.

The stats in the advertising manager may help you determine how well your ad campaign is doing. If you've already used Google AdWords or Microsoft adCenter, you're in luck: the basics of operating a Facebook CPC campaign will be second nature with only a few tweaks.

Facebook advertisements operate differently than most other forms of pay-per-click advertising. The primary distinction is the keyword algorithm that decides when an ad will show. Many pay-per-click networks depend on ad placement on keywords entered by the user in a search query. As a result, the visitor's mindset is focused on completing a job, locating information, or resolving an issue.

If your ad is intended to attract consumers who are looking for apples, it must include the word "apples" as a keyword, whether Red Delicious or Edith Smith. You can edit keywords that attract people and activate how your advertisement is seen if you create your ad for the first time (facebook marketing for beginners.docx) or use the Ads Manager after your ad has been created. In Ads Manager, tap on the campaign you wish to update. When you click on the campaign in the resulting tab, which contains more information about the campaign, a new screen appears with more specific editing options.

Facebook advertising is personalized to the profiles of users based on their likes and interests. This implies that adverts are not shown as a result of a search, but rather as a result of viewer involvement.

Using an apple as an example (if you're not already hungry), a Facebook ad for apples would show bakery contests, cookouts, and recipe tips, rather than content or user profiles interested in ice hockey, watch collections, or scuba diving. This makes Facebook ads a more appealing marketing tactic for your company — you must consider how and why someone would use your offer.

If you've created a good business model, you should be able to consider those events and plan to include those keywords in your Facebook ad.

One impression is the total number of times your ad is displayed. Impressions are a component of the CPM (cost per thousand impressions) metric and represent the range of times the ad will be shown in a network. In addition to impressions, some indicators to consider in your ad research (and Sponsored Stories) are as follows: CLICKS: The number of times a person clicks on a link in an advertisement.

CLICK-THROUGH RATE (CTR):

This is the ratio of clicks to impressions.

⬚ PRICE: The amount you pay per click (CPC) or per 1,000 impressions (CPM).

⬚ SOCIAL CTR: The number of social clicks earned divided by the number of social impressions.

⬚ SOCIAL IMPRESSIONS: Impressions displayed with the names of the user's friends who liked your profile, RSVP'd to your game, or used your app. If you are not promoting a website, case, or device, you will not see social data.

⬚ SOCIAL REACH: People who saw your ad with the names of their friends and liked your site, RSVPed to your case, or used your app. Your ad will not be socially accessible if it does not promote a Page, Event, or App.

⬚ SOCIAL Proportion: The percentage of impressions on your ad that include the names of the viewer's friends who liked your Page, RSVP'd to your event, or utilized your application. If you are not promoting a website, case, or gadget, you will not see social statistics.

⬚ Paid: The amount you paid at the time you specified.

The general public is the intended audience. The anticipated number of individuals who would be reached by your advertising or Sponsored Stories, based on your placement. You can reach out to the particular individuals who are most likely to be interested in your business or brand, thanks to Facebook's 1 billion active users.

REACH: The number of individuals who have seen your advertisements or Sponsored Stories. Facebook makes it simple for businesses to communicate with real people by allowing them to employ highly targeted advertising and Sponsored Stories. Reaching differs from impressions, which encompass numerous viewings of an advertisement.

⬜ FREQUENCY: On average, you have seen your ad several times.

⬜ RELATIONSHIPS The number of individuals that liked your Facebook page, RSVP'd to your event or activated your gadget after viewing an ad within 24 hours. You won't see data on the Connections if you don't promote a website, case, or device.

ADS MANAGER PERFORMANCE REPORTING The metrics listed above are documented in three summary reports. These reports may be exported to an Excel file, which is useful if you have an advanced analytics team that inputs data into a bespoke dashboard. If you merely want a regular summary, reports may be provided to you by e-mail.

You have the option of determining the duration of your campaign and the time.

The next 7 days, Today, Yesterday, Last 28 days, and custom time durations are all choices. If your social media team is in charge of many pages, each report may be organized by a campaign, advertising, or even Accounts.

On the left side of the Ads Manager, choose Reports. After that, choose your report style options and click the Report Generate button.

The following are the five reports: Marketing quality. This report examines and invests in views, downloads, and clickthrough rates (CTR).

Respondent by Demographic. This report gives essential demographic information about individuals who see and click on your adverts. After studying this report, you'll be able to better target your audience by optimizing your filters.

Impressions Period Events. The graph depicts the number of conversions on your Page over time (i.e. 0–24 hours, 1–7 days, or 8–28 days).

Interactions with Inline are possible. When user engagement is critical to you, this report provides insight into the performance of advertisements or Sponsored Stories for Page postings.

Feed the media. This report displays the performance of Sponsored Stories in the News Feed, including the average position inside the feed where the article was put.

The first stages in ad analysis First, choose the starting point for your advertising. This is particularly beneficial if you want to run adverts for your business, promotion, or Page regularly. Gaining an idea of how well your ad will perform in its first run may reveal what revisions or ad alterations are necessary.

The baseline data can then be used to test various aspects of the ad that increase interest in a metric. A greater CTR may be required for a certain location or demographic.

Creating a baseline and then executing a test might help you concentrate on your next effort.

You can contrast your advertisements with the CPC and CPM results. The one with the lowest of these metrics has the best cost results for clicks and impressions. You can, however, get more specific than this.

Use each of these reports to get a sense of how your ad segmentation has changed over time. For example, women may be more active on your Facebook page at night. In the morning, perhaps more active users of your Page are 20-year-old males interested in animals. Advertising is fantastic, but you must be able to segment your audience based on demographics and engagement with your Facebook page.

The Ads Manager provides methods for aligning demographics that complement your company strategy with ad outcomes. Through responder demographics, you may build responses to the following questions: Which portions have the highest CTR? Is it conceivable that certain groups react better to your adverts than others?

Is the demographic response better or worse than you anticipated? Whether you've created a baseline, you may check to see if the ad is running at full throttle as anticipated.

This is very handy when comparing one ad variant to another.

One mistake that businesses do with pay-per-click advertising is to run it continuously, similar to how an ad would appear in a newspaper.

It is feasible to run CPC advertisements in this manner, but they are intended for more specific audiences. This is especially true given how Facebook advertising is shown. Ad budgets will be squandered if they are not reviewed regularly. Take advantage of the rare opportunity to be more focused on Facebook! If you have a limited ad budget, consider cost-per-click and cost-per-print advertising as a "turbo boost" to your Facebook presence or overall digital marketing strategy.

Images over other forms of CPC advertising are unique to Facebook ads, but so is image fatigue. Images can influence whether or not a Facebook user clicks on an ad.

Your ad viewer has likely spent a significant amount of time on Facebook — Mashable estimated in 2010 that the average Facebook user spends more than seven hours per day on the social network. As a result, they will most likely see your ad several times throughout the ad's run. This can mean a lot of exposure opportunities for the ad to be memorable, but it also means that those same viewers may end up feeling like they've seen the ad too many times if the ad picture doesn't change.

Just remember that a landing page, like a CPC or banner ad, is still useful for a Facebook ad. (A landing page is a web page that consumers arrive at after clicking on an ad.)

The commercials serve as a precursor to the action you want customers to take on the landing page.

Many businesses directly link their advertising to their websites. That is not always the best practice, especially when a web page contains multiple pieces of information that can make a call to action too complex. This is a problem that can occur on blogs and e-commerce sites. A landing page contains content that is directly related to your ad. Make certain that no pop-up pages appear when someone lands on your landing page. If the landing page is a gateway to your site, make sure your main website resembles or replicates its style for a consistent look.

Remember that you may allocate funds to another network for Facebook advertisements as well as a CPC ad. That may seem too straightforward, but it may be important to provide two distinct ways for people to learn about your firm. Likes and interests are not the same as search queries, and the objective of an ad is to make your company, product, service, or even more visible.

A Site, Event, or App allows people all over Facebook to communicate with your business in a variety of ways. Ads help to raise awareness of your company's Facebook presence.

Connections tell you, after seeing your advertising, how many people connected to your company, even if they didn't click, so you know you're driving performance.

As you can see, there is plenty of data that you can access and evaluate about your Facebook ads. You may not have time to manage your advertising but make sure someone does. Consider the strength of your ad campaign to see if your message is being delivered at the appropriate volume or if your marketing strategy needs to be tweaked. The only thing worse than advertising is spending money on advertising but not taking the time to evaluate its effectiveness to improve it.

Sponsored stories are incredibly significant, and they are an excellent method for your audience members to inform their friends about your brand.

To make Sponsored Stories as successful as possible, ensure that you do things that enable your audience to take action, such as creating interest in individuals who like your Post and buying Facebook advertisements.

Use Facebook's Like Stories tool to promote these activities to help your campaign.

Make certain that your website is not overlooked. Encourage visitors to like your page and utilize Facebook's many social plug-ins to send a message to their friends. These acts may be boosted further with Sponsored Stories.

To summarize, Sponsored Stories serve as an additional layer on top of your Facebook advertising strategy. If you think your traditional Facebook advertising is successful, Sponsored Stories can help you develop a far deeper relationship with your audience and their friends about your brand (or product or service).

There is also a Wildfire software called Storyteller that is intended to give dimension to Sponsored Stories. The Storyteller app is intended to turn user input and opinions into tales based on both News Feeds and Sponsored Stories.

You may include an app link on your Facebook sites and encourage people to answer a question or share their thoughts on it. Users may then share their remarks with their Facebook friends and put them on their timelines, or they can have the comments appear as a Sponsored Story on their Facebook sites.

Conclusion:

What's next for Facebook has sparked a lot of blogospheres and social media buzz. At times, there is so much buzz that it attracts the attention of the mainstream media. Because Facebook is one of the most popular websites in the world, its users scrutinize its every action.

When new team members join or leave Facebook, especially at the project lead level, their previous experience is questioned and examined in terms of what it may indicate about Facebook's future. Aside from rumors, when a new update is launched, a team member does an interview, or an announcement is made, it spreads like wildfire via the blogosphere. If a new feature is released, a dozen or more Facebook sites will appear almost immediately, ranting about the new features. Facebook anticipates some criticism with each update, so it ignores 48 hours of comments and then listens!

This amount of scrutiny is to be anticipated as Facebook continues to expand at a breakneck rate, adding hundreds of thousands of new members every day.

As social media continues to evolve, the whole business is being scrutinized. Every action taken by a big or small social network creates a chain reaction of discussions, blog postings, media pieces, cheers, and jeers. The community immediately calms down, adjusts to the new feature set, and waits for the next tale to release. Because Facebook is the most popular social network, it is unsurprising that it receives the most attention.

In addition to the inspection of the community, you, as a marketer, should begin studying all new features as soon as they are published to see how they may be valuable to your Facebook activity. Of course, not every function will be valuable to you from a marketing standpoint. However, to understand how they may be used, you should thoroughly examine all-new features to increase your capacity to create, connect, and interact with your community.

In this book, I provide a complete review of Facebook as well as practical knowledge that can be utilized personally, professionally, and inside your organization. Several of the features are likely to have changed by the time you read this book.

It is a commonly asked subject and one that we would want to answer. We anticipate some of these questions to be addressed, just as some of the features in this book will have changed as soon as you read this chapter.

How does this affect you as a marketer? Okay, as someone who has just completed reading several hundred pages on how to get right into Facebook and start dedicating your precious time to the social network, certain business moves, particularly those involving acquisition or IPO, must pique your curiosity. Furthermore, when Facebook expands via organic growth, acquisition, or an IPO, tens of millions more users may join the social network. Many of them may be potential or current customers.

Increasing Professionalism and Control

The 35 to 55+ age range is one of Facebook's fastest-growing groups. When Facebook originally launched, the features were designed to be appealing to students. Apps such as picture sharing, video sharing, status updates, blogging, and emailing have formed the foundation of Facebook. However, as the network expands, it draws more adults who want more integrated professional tools and capabilities, as well as greater control over how and with whom they share.

Facebook responded to the need for buddy lists and more complex privacy settings for anything you post on Facebook. It's also incredibly simple to check who views each of your posts now.

Furthermore, additional professional alternatives, such as those provided by LinkedIn, should be included in Facebook. LinkedIn is the most popular professional social network ever, with over 60 million users and growing. Users may utilize LinkedIn to write reviews, create an exportable résumé, update Vcards, and publish job advertising. It also has several additional capabilities that are only available to experts. Even though Facebook will continue to grow by introducing comparable capabilities, doing so would allow it to expand its user base. It would keep Facebook users on the network longer and, as a result, trade more data with Google. It would also push Facebook to continue to differentiate itself from the rest of the pack of social networks.

EdgeRank and the News Feed

EdgeRank has grown so important that third-party organizations have been formed to review their effectiveness with it (EdgeRankChecker.com) and to determine how to improve their performance with it (PageLever.com).

Facebook intends to address how its connections and favorite sites can better disseminate content to users. Facebook recently tested a headlines feature that looked to use EdgeRank as well.

Google against Facebook

For years, Google has been the 900pound gorilla in internet marketing and online traffic, garnering the majority of all search traffic and becoming the biggest domain on the internet. Nobody appeared to be able to oppose it after easily disposing of all of its rivals, including Yahoo! and Bing and purchasing YouTube, the second most searched site on the internet.

However, Facebook and Google have been neck and neck over the last year, and Facebook may no longer seem implausible to surpass the search giant. Furthermore, Facebook's ad income is increasing, and its News Feed uses keyword algorithms to aggregate similar content.

When Facebook improves its keyword discovery capabilities and uses this kind of targeting in its advertisements, it will have overcome the final barrier to exploiting marketers for domination and earn significantly higher ROI. And this might also put Google in a frustrating position in two or three years. Google has always had a competitive edge in knowing precisely what people want right now (purchasing objective indicated by keywords), and Facebook's dominance in social media has been another. Google was unable to address the social issue enough to get significant traction, therefore if Facebook discovers keyword aim inside social activities, Facebook will triumph.

Increasing Connection Possibilities

As previously said, Facebook has the chance to establish itself as the one login throughout the internet. Facebook could also supply these websites with features that are readily connected, and people may engage with the platform on Facebook as well. The Meebo toolbar, which is utilized in various places, including TMZ and Form, is an example of this.

The Meebo toolbar enables users to access their instant messaging services, including Facebook, straight from the website where the toolbar is installed, as well as drag-and-drop picture and video sharing.

Facebook may pursue a similar strategy, but with a deeper Facebook connection. However, to accomplish this well, Facebook would need to give useful tools to website owners and their communities. If it is valuable to the website owner, maybe by giving features that would otherwise require the installation of many plugins, Facebook will consider the toolbar as having a viral impact.

Skype grew in popularity among both consumers and businesses as an instant messaging service and a low-cost means to interact with others through video, as well as a telephone service alternative.

A Never-ending Rainbow of Possibilities

Facebook can and will add a lot more functionality in the next months and years. Some of them will be updates to existing features, while many others will be whole new methods to get even more fascinated with the social network.

The forecasts we've made are just a handful of the many that we, our colleagues, and our industry make every month.

Whatever those new features are, I urge you to examine them through the eyes of a marketer. Discover how you can encourage increased usage of these applications, create a community, and connect with your followers, prospects, and customers.

Whether you use Facebook only as a personal social network to connect with friends and family, or you utilize some of the techniques in this book to help make your company a reality and grow, keep in mind that Facebook is a gadget. The true value of Facebook is how you and your friends utilize the many functions.

Facebook is an excellent platform for producing advertisements. After you've done your research, identified what your audience enjoys, developed a content strategy, attracted and maintained your audience's attention, and been paid with a rising follow-up, you can begin advertising your brand. Please keep in mind that the company's promotion comes after all of the preceding hard work.

On social channels, it is critical to provide context and participate within that context. It would be unpleasant — and uninviting — if a friendly, funny brand impact abruptly turned to the hard pitch.

Having said that, I think consumers realize that brands, as well as their goods and services, must be pushed. Because, let's face it, if you're looking for something particular, you're going to be interested in the specifics of that item. As a result, promoting your business, brand, and goods on Facebook is entirely acceptable. Nonetheless, if you want to be successful, the majority of your interactions will be focused on developing connections with your audience and establishing a reputation. When you spend 80% of your interactions enlightening and entertaining your audience, they may accept 20% promotional material as long as you stick to the structure you've previously established. So go ahead and promote your blog articles, white papers, and other marketing materials, invite your followers to special events, and offer them unique bargains and discounts in exchange for their loyalty.

Simply said, as long as communicators emphasize the personal character of communications and use a well-thought-out media plan to target the correct audience, Facebook may be a terrific medium for public relations.

THANK YOU FOR READING!!

****